CAN YOU IMAGINE A SCHOOL MISSION STATEMENT THAT PROMISED THE FOLLOWING?

- Each child's learning style will be identified and all material will be presented in a format that honors that style.

- Each child's "readiness" will be considered before he or she begins an area of learning.

- Each child will be encouraged to follow his or her interests.

- Each child will learn by doing.

- Each child will be honored as an individual.

- Each child will have downtime to play and just be a kid.

- Each child will be encouraged to pursue his or her passions in life.

- Each child's special genius will be discovered, nurtured, and preserved.

No one knows and loves your child the way you do.
So who is better qualified than you to help them learn?

HOMESCHOOLING FOR SUCCESS

"This is a splendid and valuable work in the expanding field of homeschooling, which the authors have rendered an attractive, exciting, and eminently practical adventure of the mind—
I congratulate them!"

—Joseph Chilton Pearce, author of *Magical Child* and
Evolution's End: Claiming the Potential of Our Intelligence

"This concise blend of inspiration and practical resources can guide your family to educational success . . . and fun too!"

—Linda Dobson, author of *Homeschooling: The First Year*

HOMESCHOOLING
for
SUCCESS

HOW PARENTS CAN CREATE A
SUPERIOR EDUCATION FOR THEIR CHILD

Rebecca Kochenderfer *and* Elizabeth Kanna

WARNER BOOKS

An AOL Time Warner Company

Copyright © 2002 by Rebecca Kochenderfer and Elizabeth Kanna
All rights reserved.

Warner Books, Inc., 1271 Avenue of the Americas, New York, NY 10020

Visit our Web site at www.twbookmark.com.

 An AOL Time Warner Company

Printed in the United States of America

First Printing: July 2002

10 9 8 7 6 5 4 3 2 1

Library of Congress Cataloging-in-Publication Data

Kochenderfer, Rebecca.
    Homeschooling for success : how parents can create a superior education for their child
/ Rebecca Kochenderfer and Elizabeth Kanna; with a foreword by Robert T. Kiyosaki.
        p. cm.
    Includes bibliographical references and index.
    ISBN 0-446-67885-6
    1. Homeschooling—United States. 2. Education—Parent participation—United States. I.
Kanna, Elizabeth. II. Title.

    LC40 .K63 2002
    371.04'2—dc21   2002016833

Cover design by Brigid Pearson
Book design by Charles Sutherland

For
William, David, Christina, and Madison Kochenderfer
Michael, Randall, Madison, and McKenzie Kanna
And
The early homeschooling pioneers that paved the way . . .

ACKNOWLEDGMENTS

This book could not have come to be without the incredible support we received from:

Our gifted editor, Molly Chehak, and her team at Warner Books

Our invaluable Homeschool.com team: Christopher Jaime, Sherri Smith, Patricia Malama, Jackie Grubb, and William Kochenderfer

Our mentors

Robert Kiyosaki, Kim Kiyosaki, Sharon Lechter

Also

Matthew Gollub and Linda L. Cook

And

The thousands of homeschooling families that we have had the pleasure of advising, learning from, and making a part of our lives.

CONTENTS

FOREWORD:
FOR THE LOVE OF LEARNING

I AM HONORED TO WRITE THE FOREWORD FOR this book on homeschooling, because this is a book for parents who are taking an active role in their child's education. My own success story can be attributed to such parents. I graduated from school and have done relatively well in life simply because my dad took an active role in my education and encouraged my love of learning.

My first book *Rich Dad, Poor Dad* is really a book about homeschooling, in the sense that it is about a parent's influence on a child's overall success in life. My real dad—the man I call my poor dad—was a schoolteacher, and eventually the head of education for the state of Hawaii. When I began failing in school—the very system he presided over—he took a more active interest in my academic education. Similarly, my best friend's father—the man I call my rich dad—took an active interest in my financial education. In retrospect, I realize that my *report card of life* has been more greatly influenced by my two dads than all the education I received in school. The combination of these two individuals' involvement in my education is responsible for my success in life.

Public school was a frightening and often humiliating place for me. As a mature adult, the only recurring nightmare I have is a dream in which I'm taking a test I was not prepared for, knowing I was going to fail. School for me simply meant long hours of boredom. I had very little interest in the subjects I was required to study. At PTA meetings, my parents were often told that I was "slow," "lacking motivation," and "not applying myself." Despite these labels, I knew I was not stupid. I was simply bored and could find very little relationship between what I was studying and real life. If I were in school today, I would probably be labeled as someone with a learning disability such as ADD or ADHD. I would be the poster boy for Ritalin.

At the age of fifteen, I flunked out of high school. It was the single most painful experience in my life up to that point. As the superintendent of education for the state of Hawaii, my father was certainly less than thrilled to have his son flunking school. Word spread quickly among his colleagues, and there were a few jokes about the top educator's son being a scholastic failure. I don't know if my dad was embarrassed, but if he was, he didn't show it. All he said when he came home the night I received my failing grade was "It's time for your education to begin." And begin it did.

Even though my father ran the school system, he knew it could never replace the lessons taught by a child's parents. He decided to step in and take an active role in my education. He did not focus on grades, passing tests, class ranking, which college I was going to, or how high my IQ was. The first thing he focused on was restoring my love of learning, which had been badly damaged. His lessons began when he said, "Learn to study because you want to learn, not because you have to pass a test." He also said, "Sometimes in life, we need to learn things we may not want to learn. So before you begin studying anything, even if you do not want to study it, first find out why you want to learn whatever it is you are studying. Learning how to want to learn is more important than the grades you receive."

Although I never learned to like school, my parents' intervention in my education helped me graduate. I was even awarded a congressional appointment to an academically tough military college in New York from which I graduated with a bachelor of science degree. Recently, at my thirtieth college class reunion, I caught up with old friends and reminisced about the times when we were young and looking forward to our future. It was interesting to see who had aged the most, who was still thin, who gained the most weight, who was successful, married, divorced, had kids, grandkids, and who was no longer alive. The reunion inspired me to reflect back on all of life's successes and failures. I realized that most of my success did not come from what I learned in school, but from what I learned at home.

Today, I continue to be a poor reader, yet I read because I want to learn. I continue to be a poor writer, yet I have had four books on the *Wall Street Journal* bestseller list. I managed to graduate from high school in spite of the fact that nearly 50 percent of those who started with me failed along the way—and many of those had had higher SAT scores, higher grade point averages, and higher IQs than I did. Talking to my classmates at my reunion in New York helped me realize that where we are today has very little to do with how well we did in school but more to do with how well we did at home, both as children and as adults.

In closing, I will leave you with words of wisdom from both my rich dad and poor dad, words of wisdom that have helped me with my report card of life. May these words assist you in guiding your children's education and preparing them for the world they will face as adults.

As my schoolteacher dad once said to me, "Life is not about grades. Life is about lifelong learning."

Thank you for reading this very important book.

—Robert Kiyosaki

INTRODUCTION

IF YOU ARE READING THIS, YOU ARE AT LEAST CURIOUS about homeschooling. Perhaps you've heard how the number of homeschooling families is growing or you have met a family that homeschools. Maybe you're researching homeschooling out of desperation because of your child's school situation. Regardless of the reasons that compelled you to pick up this book, we want to share with you one important message: You *can* successfully homeschool your child.

Trust us. We have successfully homeschooled our own children, as have over two million families across America. We are not rocket scientists by profession. We don't have unlimited amounts of patience, and we do get mad and frustrated with our kids sometimes. We don't get up at six A.M. to clean our whole house before we start homeschooling for the day (although we admire those who do). We can't cook dinner and help our kids with a messy science experiment at the same time (oops, yes, we can do that). We don't turn every second of the day into a teachable moment. And we do occasionally dream about our before-children days—days spent reading the *entire* Sunday paper in bed. In other words, we are probably a lot like you, with one big exception: Our children have never crossed a public school threshold. Our years of observation and knowledge of how our children learn best allowed us to create a superior education for them at home.

Although our children have not yet reached adulthood, they are happy, confident, intelligent self-starters who love to learn. Whether or not our children receive a full ride to Harvard, Dartmouth, or Yale, as many other homeschoolers*

---

*The term "homeschooler" refers to both the homeschooled children and the parents who homeschool.

have before them, we and our spouses believe that our children's home education is preparing them to meet all the challenges and opportunities that life will present to them. The education they receive at home is superior because it follows one fundamental belief, and we use this one belief as our guiding principal in all aspects of our children's education: Each of our children was born with special gifts and talents. Each of them was born with his or her own unique genius. Homeschooling is the best educational option for us to honor those special gifts because it can be tailored to each of our children's learning styles, interests, readiness, and intelligence.

The customized nature of homeschooling has led to many outstanding achievements by homeschoolers, many of whom have been in the media spotlight and are profiled throughout this book. While many educators consider customized learning or one-on-one learning as an optimal learning environment for a child's future success, we believe it is every child's birthright. So, why did the two of us decide to homeschool our kids?

My (Elizabeth Kanna's) husband, a public junior high school teacher, first brought the subject of homeschooling to my attention in 1992, when our first child was three. I thought he was joking. Homeschool? That was for weirdos! What kind of a person wouldn't send their kids to school? I had plenty of objections to homeschooling, but after reading *Homeschooling for Excellence* by David and Micki Colfax (one of the first books on homeschooling ever published), I was hooked. I loved the idea of helping our inquisitive daughter learn about the world. We had so much fun together. Did it all have to end when our daughter turned five? Couldn't we continue as we were now? Ten years and two more daughters later, my children continue to learn at home.

Our girls are encouraged to approach new subjects and milestones in their life when they are ready, not when society says they should. Rather than impeding their emotional and social progress, I believe homeschooling has put our girls ahead of the curve. My oldest daughter, Randall, recently had the opportunity to meet and interview Dr. Robert Ballard, the man who found the *Titanic*. Even though she was only eleven years old, she was poised and articulate when interviewing this world-renowned scientist, demonstrating skill far beyond her chronological age and public school–educated peers.

I (Rebecca Kochenderfer) was motivated to homeschool my children by the same reason I became a special education teacher: I loved seeing the spark in children's eyes when they learned something new. I wanted to be the one to see the spark in my own children's eyes when they learned to read or learned how to add numbers for the first time. But my foremost homeschooling goal is to help my children develop their natural gifts. For example, my son is a hands-on learner, and homeschooling has provided us with the freedom to make sure he has plenty of opportunities to build things, explore, and create mad science experiments.

Like many homeschooling parents, homeschooling became not only an educational choice for us, it became a lifestyle—a lifestyle based on freedom and flexibility. My husband and I made traveling a priority in our lives before we started our family and we wanted to continue to travel after our children were born. The flexibility of homeschooling gives us the opportunity to show our children as much of the world as we can and still provide them with a good education.

GET READY—YOUR LIFE IS GOING TO CHANGE

Homeschooling has the power to change your life. It has certainly changed ours. Even though you choose to homeschool for your children's benefit, something amazing happens to you, the parent. You get excited about learning again. You may remember how much you liked reading historical novels, or rediscover how much you liked science, or you decide to take guitar lessons, too, when you sign up your child for lessons. You start to see all the possibilities that life has to offer again—just like a child does. As we continue to help our children explore their special talents, we have simultaneously rediscovered our own talents.

For us, the fact that we could do something "radical" like homeschooling and succeed gave us the confidence to try other new things. One sunny afternoon in

January, while our kids ran around and played, we conceived the idea for an on-line community for all homeschooling families. We envisioned a portal that would help families find the information and support we wished we had had when we started homeschooling our children. Three months later, we launched Homeschool.com. Three years later, Homeschool.com has become not just the number one homeschooling site on the Internet, but one of the top forty-five sites on the Internet, according to *Forbes* magazine. Through Homeschool.com we have helped thousands of homeschoolers across the United States and have worked with some of the leading voices in the homeschooling community. We believe we have discovered the secrets to successful homeschooling and, in fact, to a superior education. This book is intended to share those secrets.

In this book, we don't draw upon just our own personal homeschooling experiences but the experiences of thousands of homeschooling families. We also provide information, support, and resources for all different styles and approaches to homeschooling. As founders of Homeschool.com, we have had the opportunity to meet or interview some of the most respected Ph.D.'s, best-selling authors, educators, scientists, historians, and mathematicians, as well as other home-schooling experts. That experience and knowledge is shared with you in this book.

We wrote this book because homeschooling has had a profound effect on our lives and on our children's lives. So, for a few hours, a few days, or maybe forever, forget about what society dictates is "the right way" for your child to be educated and consider looking "outside the box" for your child's education. We did. And we wrote this book so that you can look outside the box and create a superior education for your children at home too.

THE TEN MOST IMPORTANT THINGS YOU NEED TO KNOW ABOUT HOMESCHOOLING

1. Homeschooling is life changing. It creates personal growth for both the parent and the child. You (the parent) get a chance to re-

discover your own special genius while you help your children discover theirs. Nothing you will ever do will have a more profound effect on your child and your family's future as homeschooling.

2. You are qualified to homeschool your children if you love to read to them, love to spend time with them, love to explore the world with them, love to see them learn new things, and, most important, love them.

3. Children love to learn. It is as natural to them as breathing. They have an inborn hunger to explore the world and examine what is interesting. They learn by following their interests, with one interest leading to another. This is the way we all learned as younger children and how as adults we learn after we leave school. Homeschooling families learn together and know that learning is a lifelong process.

4. Homeschooling is legal everywhere in the United States, but homeschooling laws vary from state to state. The three basic categories for homeschooling laws are: home education laws, private school laws, and equivalency laws. (See Appendix C for the laws in your state.)

5. It does not take six to eight hours a day to homeschool your child. Most of the time children spend at school consists of waiting. Design a plan that works for your family and be prepared to scratch it several times and start over. Don't sacrifice your family's happiness to "school" your children. There are many ways families homeschool; find what works for you and your family.

6. Your child will not become a social misfit. Children do not need to be socialized in a large group of same-age children to become well-adjusted socially. Quite the opposite. Most parents want their children to learn their social graces from adults, not other chil-

dren. Homeschoolers have healthy relationships with people of all ages, including the new mother next door; the retired couple who loves to garden; their friends at ballet, 4-H, and karate; and, most important, their parents.

7. You will not have to teach algebra unless you really want to. It is not necessary to teach pre-algebra to ten-year-olds. When your teen decides to become a scientist, or is ready to explore the requirements of college admission, together you will explore the ways they can learn algebra: in a community college class, with a tutor, or through textbooks. After years of using math in their daily lives, homeschooled teens are well equipped to teach themselves higher math. Don't worry about it when they are ten.

8. You will question yourself a lot. Maybe several times a day in the beginning. This is normal. Find a fellow homeschooling friend. Support each other. Tell each other that it's okay to sometimes feel that your children didn't seem to learn anything on a given day. They did, and so did you!

9. You do not have to starve or live in a tent to homeschool your children. Thousands of homeschooling families are able to make the money they need and homeschool their children at the same time. While you create a family business or dream job, or restructure your current job, your children will learn the most important skill of all—how to create the life of their dreams.

10. Trust in your child. They learned how to love, smile, crawl, walk, talk, run, dress themselves, and understand their world before starting school, and they will continue to grow and learn without school.

CHAPTER ONE

Home: The Ideal School

Joanne sits in school each day, waiting. If only she could tell her teacher all the things she is thinking about, then her teacher would know how smart she is! Her mom and dad tell her all the time how smart she is and that she is a great artist; her grandmother says she is a genius. But if she's so smart, how come her teacher never tells her so? How come her teacher never calls on her to answer a question in class? If she is smart, why does she have a hard time learning things in class? Joanne loves art, and often day-dreams about creating beautiful pictures, but she rarely gets to draw in class, and the last time she did, her teacher told her what to draw. She really wanted to draw a pic-ture of those fluffy clouds she saw that morning on the way to school. Instead, she was told to find all the words that begin with a "B" on a worksheet and then color them blue. She was given only a blue crayon. She knew if she colored a cloud blue on the worksheet, her teacher would not be pleased. She is also distracted by all the interrup-tions while trying to read in class, and she really does not like the story her teacher gives her to read anyway. She likes stories about little girls like her, but ones who lived a long time ago like the Little House on the Prairie *books her mom reads to her. Her mom is also teaching her how to cook. She gets to touch everything . . . and measure stuff! At the end of the school day, she can't wait to get home and draw some pictures and do some more cooking with her mom. But she almost always has homework. After her homework is done, it is time for dinner and then it is bedtime. If only she could stay up a little later with her mom and dad, but tomorrow is another school day.*

Joanne is six years old. She will spend the next eleven years in compulsory classrooms—eleven more years in classrooms that don't teach to her personal learning style. Classrooms that are distracting, crowded, and often boring. Classrooms that will do little to encourage her love of learning. Classrooms where her intelligence, interests, and talents will most likely never be recognized, much less nurtured.

What would happen if Joanne learned at home, where her love of learning has been encouraged since the day she was born? At home, she could have learned by touching and doing, where her paintings of fluffy clouds could cover her bedroom walls, and where she could have spent more time with the people who love her more than anyone else in the world.

> "Government schooling is the most radical adventure in history. It kills the family by monopolizing the best times of childhood and by teaching disrespect for home and parents."
>
> John Taylor Gatto,
> *The Underground History of American Education*

Homeschooling is not new. It is the way this country has educated its children for all but the last 150 years. Now, at the beginning of the twenty-first century, as many as two million children in the United States are learning at home. Why the resurgence of such an educational method? Because homeschooling *is* the ideal school for most children, and one that our current schools won't *ever* be able to compete with.

CREATING DRONES

Our public schools were designed on a factory principal: assembly line education to create conformist citizens. The ultimate one-size-fits-all. In the industrial age, the United States needed millions of workers for the assembly lines. Our public schools were designed to create factory drones who would follow instructions, without asking too many questions. While these schools achieved their goal in the early industrial age, the standard of education they established is no longer socially or economically relevant. We live in an age that requires higher standards and increased creativity. The industrial revolution is over.*

> "The part of the brain that thrives on worksheets and teacher lectures probably takes up less than one percent of the total available for learning."
>
> Thomas Armstrong, Ph.D., *In Their Own Way*

CREATING INDIVIDUALS

In his recent book, *The Roaring 2000s*, Harry S. Dent, Jr., one of the world's most prescient economic prognosticators, describes the ideal school of the future: "Teachers must . . . cultivate a relationship with each individual student. They must determine exactly where each child is in the development process and their specific strengths and weaknesses in learning. They must give each child the individual attention he or she needs to feel valued as a human being, which generates self-esteem and motivation. By establishing a personal relationship with each child, the teacher can determine which subjects and skills need emphasis at each stage of education. They can protect children from the often cruel criticism of

*For more on this, read: *Coloring Outside the Lines* by Roger Shank (HarperCollins, 2000).

others by not putting them into classes and learning experiences for which they are not ready."

Dent's vision of an ideal school in the future will be one in which a child's uniqueness is honored—an idea that runs counter to the principles of our schools. We do not honor the "crazy ideas" kids have. We simply can't honor the individual in a classroom of thirty kids. The teacher does not have time. She has to keep the class moving: They must be on lesson twelve before the third week of the second semester to keep up with the state's standards.

Some might think that honoring the individual sounds "new agey" and not really important in preparing children for success. But honoring each child's uniqueness is not only what all children deserve, it is critical to their future success.

The world our children will function in as adults is a world we have never seen before—from where they will live and how they will communicate to the new business model they will utilize. And in this new world, the most highly valued skills will be creativity and uniqueness—both entrepreneurial and interpersonal. What type of education has the power to create these skills in children? Customized education. According to Dent, this is the only education that will help our children develop the skills they will need for success in the information age. Can a school that serves up a one-size-fits-all curriculum deliver a customized education to children? Of course not. What Dent calls "our top-down, left-brain, mass educational system" cannot give children the individualized education they need. Harry Dent is not alone in his vision of a school of the future that honors the individual and provides an education customized to that uniqueness.

Howard Gardner, a Harvard University psychologist, identified in *Frames of Mind* seven different geniuses or intelligences in 1983. Gardner's theory of the existence of seven different intelligences (and his refined theory of an eighth intelligence in 1996) has become one of the most discussed and inspirational theories of the twentieth century.* In his recent book, *Intelligence Reframed*, Gardner

---

*Gardner's eight intelligences are detailed in Chapter Seven.

shares his vision of an education that honors a child's unique range of intelligences. Gardner labels it "individually configured education," and describes it as "education that takes individual differences seriously and, insofar as possible, crafts practices that serve different kinds of minds equally well." To provide this customized learning environment, teachers must learn about each student's background, interests, and goals. Gardner and Dent's vision of an ideal school are very similar to other well-known educators, experts, Ph.D.'s, and theorists. Many are using their books, programs, and public forums to reach parents, educators, and legislators. Their cumulative message is clear: We must reform our current one-size-fits-all educational system now.

In 1977, John Holt launched a magazine seen by many as "radical" for the seventies, especially considering the author's professional background. John Holt was a devoted teacher and bestselling author of two books about school reform published in the sixties (he was to write ten during his lifetime). He hoped his books would be a catalyst for school reform. For many years he tried to reform schools through his writing and talking as an educator. But his message of how children really learn and how schools must honor the individual in each child fell on deaf ears in the very system he worked in and wanted to help reform. It was very hard both personally and professionally for Holt to give up his mission of reforming schools, but after many years he came to the conclusion that the task was impossible and began to advocate homeschooling. He created *Growing Without Schooling* to bypass schools and talk directly to parents. Holt felt parents could create an education at home that honored how children really learn after he saw firsthand how many homeschooling families were doing just that. Is the task impossible for our school system? Many educators believe that teaching to each child's learning style, intelligence, and interests would be virtually impossible in our current school system.

Bureaucrats, textbooks publishers, and other education companies have large stakes in our current school system. The massive changes that would be required of schools to enable them to provide customized education to each and every child are enormous. The chances of it happening in our lifetime are small. Will it happen? Only time will tell.

Given the limited choices available for finding a customized education for your child in a public or private school, how can you create one at home? One that encourages a lifelong love of learning, where the subjects and materials to be covered are appropriate for their readiness and skill level, and where your child feels valued as a human being? Most likely you have already created it.

THE IDEAL SCHOOL

Can you imagine a school mission statement that promises the following?

- Each child's learning style will be identified and all material will be presented in a format that honors that style.
- Each child's "readiness" will be considered before he begins an area of learning.
- Each child will be encouraged to follow her interests.
- Each child will learn by doing.
- Each child will be honored as an individual.
- Each child will have downtime to play and just be a kid.
- Each child will be encouraged to pursue his passion in life.
- Each child's special genius will be discovered, nurtured, and preserved.

A school that can deliver these educational standards *does* exist. Families across the country have created this ideal school right in their homes. And you can too.

Since the day your child was born, you have been helping him learn. You knew his signals, he did not have to be able to speak, you just knew. You helped him learn how to walk, talk, feed himself and explore his world. You naturally knew when to challenge him a bit and when to let nature take its course. You've been answering his questions since he was old enough to ask them. You've helped him explore the world with a constant eye on building his self-confidence during his explorations. It is said that human beings learn more during their first five years of life than at any other time. Why, then, when our children reach the age of five, do we automatically assume we are no longer qualified to help them learn? Our society has done a very good job convincing parents that "experts" must take over after their child is of school age. This long-held belief goes back to a time in our history when most parents had no education and could not even help their children learn basic skills such as reading and writing. This is no longer the case. With parents' instinctive desire to help their children learn, the vast amounts of educational products available for home use, and resources for determining how children learn best, parents can provide an education for their child at home that far exceeds what is available in any private or public school.

The facts about homeschooling speak for themselves:

Homeschooled children are outperforming their conventionally schooled peers. According to a recent cover story in *Time* magazine, ". . . the average SAT score for home schoolers in 2000 was 1100, compared with 1019 for the general population. And a large study by University of Maryland education researcher Lawrence Rudner showed that the average home schooler scored in the 75th percentile on the Iowa Test of Basic Skills; the 50th percentile marked the national average. . . ." Today Harvard admissions officers attend homeschooling conferences looking for applicants, and Rice and Stanford admit home schoolers at rates equal to or higher than those for public schoolers.*

As you read this book, you will gain confidence in your abilities to homeschool your child. Remember, other parents (just like you) are homeschooling their children, and you are just as qualified as they are.

At first you may lack confidence in your abilities to teach and in your child's ability to learn. But remember that you were your child's first teacher and you are

*John Cloud and Jodie Morse. "Is Home Schooling Good for America?" *Time* (August 27, 2001).

still their best. No one cares about your child as much as you or knows her as well as you do. Many homeschooling parents have discovered that making the choice to homeschool and succeeding at it has taught them to trust themselves and given them the confidence to try other endeavors. Homeschooling is not for everyone, but for two million families in the United States, homeschooling has become not just an education, it has become a lifestyle where individuality is respected and strong family bonds are created.

All parents share the universal belief that their child was born with special talents and gifts, their own special genius. Use that belief as your guiding principle as you create a superior education for your child in the ideal school—your home.

CHAPTER TWO

Questions and Answers About Homeschooling

SINCE YOU'RE READING THIS BOOK, you're obviously excited about exploring homeschooling. But with the excitement come doubts and questions. Home-schooling sounds easy, but how can it be easy? What about teaching algebra or, worse, chemistry? Won't my child become a social misfit? Does my family have to be Christian, or start eating tofu and living on a mountaintop to homeschool?

- Homeschooling is legal in all fifty states.
- There are two million homeschoolers in the United States.
- Homeschooling costs between $500 and $2,000 per child per year.
- A few states have charter schools that help pay for homeschooling.
- Homeschooled children score higher on academic tests than do public and private school students.
- Homeschoolers do well on socialization evaluations.
- You can work *and* homeschool your children.
- You can homeschool if you're in the military.
- You can homeschool if you're a single parent.

Homeschool.com has helped thousands of parents make an informed decision about homeschooling, and the most frequently asked questions that most new-to-homeschooling parents have are answered in this chapter. Read them all or choose the ones that answer your specific questions. But remember these two things: (1) having doubts and a lot of questions is normal, and (2) don't let your doubts stop you from exploring this incredible option for you and your children. Most likely, you attended a conventional school as a child and not having your children go to school is different. Different can be confusing and scary even when it feels right and makes sense. Keep reading and you will have the information and confidence to make an informed decision about homeschooling.

This chapter provides an overview of the issues homeschoolers face. Each issue receives in-depth treatment in subsequent chapters, so use this FAQ list as a road map for the rest of the book. It will direct you to the issue of most concern to you. However, regardless of the age of your child, reading all chapters will benefit you. Even if your child is of high school age, you might want to read the history and science sections in the early years chapter (Chapter Four) since the information is important for older children too. Or if you have a younger child who is just beginning her formal education, we would suggest that you read the college chapter too. Hopefully, it will encourage you and put your fears to rest that if you homeschool your child she won't be able to attend college.

Q: What is homeschooling?

A: Homeschooling is the most flexible and diverse educational option available today. The variety of homeschooling styles reflects the diversity of the people who choose this method. Some families organize their homeschool the same as a traditional school, with the children studying the same subjects the same way as public school students. Some families use the opposite approach and "un-school" their children—a far less structured approach where the children's schedule is determined by their interests and readiness. Most homeschoolers, however, use an eclectic approach that is partly structured and partly interest-based. This method allows parents to pick and choose the classes and materials that meet their children's needs. These may be college or co-op classes, pool teaching, charter schools, independent study programs, apprenticeships, volunteering, and a host of other options. Homeschooling is as unique as you are.

Q: What type of families homeschool their children?

A: Although homeschoolers are often stereotyped as hippies or religious fanatics, most homeschoolers are just normal parents who have decided to take charge of their children's education. Homeschoolers are everywhere and come from all walks of life. They live in cities, in the suburbs, and in the country. They are doctors and janitors and public school teachers. Some homeschoolers have strong religious beliefs and some are nonbelievers. Homeschoolers are just like you.

What do these people have in common?

Jason Taylor (Miami Dolphins defensive end)
Duane "Digger" Carey (astronaut)
Hanson (popular singing group)
Venus and Serena Williams (tennis champions)
Garth Brooks (singer)
Lisa Whelchel (actress)
Rick Santorum (United States senator from Pennsylvania)
Aaron Fessler (sold his business, Allegro, for $55 million)
Sean Conley (first place winner, 2001 National Spelling Bee)
Todd Lodwick (member United States ski team)
Kitty Gilmore (United States marshal)
Peter Kindersley (founder of Dorling Kindersley publishers)
Ansel Adams (photographer)
William F. Buckley (author/lecturer/speaker)
LeAnn Rimes (country singer)

All of these individuals were either homeschooled themselves or homeschool(ed) their children.

Q: **Is homeschooling legal?**

A: Homeschooling is legal in all fifty states and throughout Canada. Homeschooling is also becoming increasingly popular in Australia, New Zealand, England, and Japan. However, every state and province has its own laws regarding homeschooling and some are more "friendly" than others. Some homeschooling laws merely require you to let your local school district know that you will be homeschooling your children. Some laws require you to fill out paperwork as if you were a private school. If you are considering homeschooling, you will need to get information on the current laws in your area. State or local homeschool groups are often the best source of information. To learn more about the laws in your state, see Appendix C.

Q: **Why do families choose to homeschool?**

A: Families homeschool for a variety of different reasons. In the past, most families homeschooled for religious reasons, but now more and more families are choosing to homeschool for academic reasons and because they are concerned about the drugs, violence, and negative peer pressure so common in schools today. They also want to spend more time together as a family. Interestingly, teens are increasingly choosing to direct their own learning and have been contacting Homeschool.com seeking advice on how to convince their parents to homeschool them. Most of these young people are deeply unhappy with school and want the chance to explore something different. Regardless of the motivation, homeschooling parents are united by the same belief—a belief that they can do a better job educating their children than the schools can.

Q: **How many families choose to homeschool?**

A: The number of homeschoolers is estimated to be between 1.23 million and 2 million. It is the fastest growing trend in education, growing at a rate of 15 percent each year.*

*These statistics were published in a 1997 study by Dr. Brian Ray of the National Home Education Research Institute, and also in a *Wall Street Journal*/NBC News poll published in March 1997.

Q: **How much does homeschooling cost?**

A: Depending on the choices you make, homeschooling can cost either a little or a lot. Generally, you can assume that homeschooling costs more than a public school education and less than a private school. If you had to, you could homeschool for free using public resources like libraries, PBS shows, museums, the Internet, and hand-me-down educational supplies.

In general, homeschooling costs more if you use a boxed curriculum or sign up with an independent study program. For example, in 2001, a complete fifth-grade program costs $570 from Calvert School, $230 from Alpha Omega Publications, $550 from Clonlara, and $1,400 from Laurel Springs. Homeschooling costs are higher for teenagers than for elementary school students, and fees are normally charged on a per unit basis. Since many homeschool teens also take college classes, you will have to factor that into your educational budget.

You will also want to budget additional funding for extracurricular activities such as soccer, gymnastics, martial arts, piano lessons, and the like. Since homeschooled children have more time, they tend to participate in more of these activities.

The bottom line is that: (1) you have complete control over how much homeschooling will cost and (2) you can give your child a quality education no matter how much or how little money you have.

Q: **Can I work and homeschool my child too?**

A: Absolutely. Although many homeschooling families do have one parent who stays home full-time, many other parents have found ways to bring in an income *and* homeschool their children. Thousands of families have started small businesses, created a virtual office, found telecommuting positions or flextime work, and created the income they needed while homeschooling their children. The world is changing. Technologies like the Internet, cellular telephones, and portable computers are changing the way business is done, and this is creating more flexible employment options than ever before. Chapter Eight has information on telecommuting, flextime, job sharing, part-time work, and saving money (so you don't have to work). With a little creativity, you can find a great job or start a business that allows you to work from home and homeschool your children.

Q: **What are the advantages of homeschooling?**

A: For many homeschoolers, one of the greatest benefits of homeschooling is the strengthening of family bonds. Homeschooling families spend lots of time learning and playing together and this naturally creates close ties between brothers and sisters and between children and parents. Homeschoolers also have a great deal of flexibility in how and what they learn, allowing them to learn about the "real world" by being part of it. These advantages allow homeschooled children to receive a superior education that is attuned specifically to their own needs, learning style, personality, and interests.

Q: **What are the disadvantages in homeschooling?**

A: According to homeschoolers' feedback on Homeschool.com, the biggest disadvantage facing the homeschooling family is loss of income. Someone must be home, at least part-time, to facilitate the children's learning. At a time when it can often be difficult to get by on two incomes, it can be a real challenge to get by on just one. Chapter Eight explores the different ways to handle this potential loss of income. Some of the other difficulties facing homeschooling parents include lack of confidence in their own and their children's abilities, public and/or family criticism, and adjusting career goals and work schedules to accommodate the needs of the family. One last challenge humorously cited by homeschoolers is that of housekeeping. When you use your home full-time for homeschooling (and in some cases even for work), things can get a bit messy. But don't worry, those books piled high on the coffee table, the science experiment on the table, and the art project in the patio are all signs that your child is learning.

Q: **How do homeschooled children perform academically?**

A: Although many homeschoolers do not believe that standardized tests adequately reflect a child's intelligence, homeschoolers do well on these tests and routinely outperform both publicly and privately schooled students.

- A 1988 Tennessee study reported that homeschoolers scored in the 83rd percentile in reading and 77th percentile in math. (Fifty percent is considered to be an average score.)
- A 1988 Oregon study found that 73 percent of homeschool students who were tested scored above average.
- In 1989 homeschoolers in Washington state scored at the 66th percentile on the Stanford Achievement Test, scoring highest in science, listening, vocabulary, and reading.
- In 1990 homeschoolers in Montana scored at the 72nd percentile on that state's standardized achievement tests.
- In 1992, homeschoolers in Pennsylvania scored at the 86th percentile in reading and the 73rd percentile in math.
- In 1994, 16,311 conservative Christian homeschoolers were tested using the Iowa Test of Basic Skills. These homeschoolers scored in the 77th percentile on the Basic Battery (which tests reading, language, and math), the 73rd percentile in language, and the 73rd percentile in math.
- In a 1997 nationwide study, the National Home Education Research Institute collected data on 5,402 students from 1,657 families. In this study the students scored in the 87th percentile in reading, 80th percentile in language, and 82nd percentile in math.
- According to ACT achievement test reports, while the average composite score of American high school students taking the ACT test was 21, homeschooled teens scored 22.8 (out of a possible 36).
- Homeschoolers placed highest on the SAT college entrance exams in the year 2000.
- Homeschoolers took first, second, and third place in the 2000 Scripps-Howard national spelling bee.

- Homeschoolers placed first and third in the 1999 and 2000 National Geographic Society geography bees, respectively.
- In a 1999 study commissioned by the Home School Legal Defense Association (HLSDA), about 25 percent of all homeschooled students are enrolled one or more grades above their age level, with the achievement gap widening as students progress. By the eighth grade, the average homeschool student performs four grade levels above the national average.

Q: **How are homeschooled students doing socially?**

A: It used to be that if you announced that you were going to homeschool your children people would ask you, "How will your children learn anything?" Now that fears have been put to rest regarding homeschoolers' academic achievement, the most commonly asked question is, "But what about socialization?" The assumption is that children will not learn to get along with others and will not develop good social skills unless they go to school. However, several studies have been conducted over the years that show that homeschooled children are more self-confident and less peer dependent than traditionally schooled students.

According to research:

- A 1986 study found that homeschooled students have significantly higher self-concepts than their conventionally schooled peers.
- A 1986 study found homeschooled students less peer dependent than private school students.
- A 1989 study found that homeschoolers were just as involved in out-of-school and extracurricular activities that predict leadership in adulthood as were those who attended private schools.
- A 1991 study concluded homeschooling parents carefully address the socialization needs of their children in every area studied (i.e., personal identity, personal destiny, values and moral development, autonomy, relationships, sexuality, and social skills).

- A 1991 study looked at adults who were homeschooled. None was unemployed and none was on welfare; 94 percent said homeschooling prepared them to be independent; 79 percent said it helped them interact with individuals from different levels of society, and they strongly supported homeschooling.
- A 1992 study found homeschoolers had significantly lower problem behavior scores than do conventional school students.

Many people believe that homeschoolers spend all their time around the kitchen table, but that simply is not the case. Since homeschooled students do not spend six hours a day in a classroom sitting behind a desk, they have more time to participate in activities outside the home like music, sports, and Scouts. Also, whereas schoolchildren rarely have the opportunity to interact with children who are not the same age, homeschooled children interact with and learn from people of all ages, genders, and interests.

Q: Will my child be able to get into college if they are homeschooled?

A: Homeschoolers are accepted and recruited by some of the top universities in the country because of their maturity, independent thinking skills, creativity, and strong academic preparation. As previously mentioned, homeschoolers perform above average on the ACT. Success on the ACT test reveals that the courses taken by high school students to prepare for college have been effective. Homeschoolers also placed highest on the SAT college entrance exams in the year 2000. In addition to academic success, homeschoolers have had athletic success in college. Coaches are recruiting homeschooled athletes, and in 2001 the National Collegiate Athletic Association (NCAA) declared about 100 homeschooled students eligible for athletics as freshmen at major universities, up from 85 a year ago. An article in *Time* on September 11, 2000, reported that 26 percent of 35 homeschooled applicants had been accepted into Stanford University's 2000–2001 freshman class. This is nearly double the rate of overall acceptance. For more information about homeschoolers and college, see Chapter Six.

Q: **Will my children be able to succeed in the "real world" if they do not go to school?**

A: Those exploring homeschooling for the first time sometimes worry that their child will not be able to function in the "real world" if they don't attend school and have the same social experiences as schooled children. But what do schools really do? They separate kids by age and ability, reinforce class and gender, and limit children's interactions to short recess periods. Schoolchildren are forced to socialize with children only their own age and are trapped in a room six to seven hours a day, allowed to view the outside world only through a textbook. Where in the real world are adults forced to socialize with only someone their own age? Competition, bullying, consumerism, and cruel teasing are often the social values children learn at school. Homeschooled children are more likely to base their decisions on values they learned from their parents instead of feeling compelled to go along with the crowd and accept the behavior of what other children are displaying as the "norm." Because homeschoolers spend so much time out in the real world, they are able to communicate well and get along with both adults and children. They even get along with their siblings, and it is common for homeschooling families to receive positive comments about their children's strong, warm sibling relationships.

Q: **What is a typical homeschooling day like?**

A: Each family's typical day is different and reflects the homeschooling style that family is using. For example, some families use a school-at-home approach, where they study the same subjects as the schools, using textbooks and tests. Some families set up their homeschool like a Waldorf or Montessori school and their typical day might begin with a candle ceremony and end with arts and crafts or organic gardening. Other families may choose a homeschooling style that emphasizes nature studies or volunteer work or natural learning. The choice is up to you. Chapter Three, Getting Started, describes the various styles homeschoolers are currently using and has a sample schedule for each style. This will help you develop a style that is right for you and your family.

Q: **How do I find textbooks and other learning materials?**

A: There are lots of educational resources to choose from. If you wanted to, you could homeschool your children using only libraries, museums, PBS shows, field trips, and the Internet. There are also hundreds of educational supply catalogues available that provide quality learning materials specifically designed for home use. The Homeschooling Resource Guide, at the end of the book, includes a list of educational suppliers. Send for the catalogues from companies that look interesting to you. They are filled with resources you may find helpful. The Homeschooling Resource Guide also has a list of curriculum suppliers and correspondence courses. Homeschooling conferences and learning fairs are another place for looking at materials and getting ideas. Finally, Homeschool.com's "Getting Started" kit includes a complete selection of education catalogues and flyers for you to explore. Don't worry about being able to find good materials for your children. Homeschooling is a lucrative market for educational companies, so consequently there is an incredible amount of educational supplies available, specifically designed for home use.

Q: **How do I teach subjects like advanced math, advanced science, or languages?**

A: You do not have to know everything to homeschool your children. If you don't know advanced math or chemistry or a particular foreign language you can look to your community for help. Perhaps your child can learn that subject using a tutor or by taking a class at the community college or on the Internet. Perhaps you have a friend who is knowledgeable in this area and would like to trade teaching with you—you teach his child pottery and he teaches your child geometry. You may even want to tackle this subject along with your child and learn something new yourself. Remember, too, that many children are able to teach themselves; just as adults do when they discover something new they want to learn. See Chapter Five for more information on pool teaching and other techniques.

Q: **How do I know what to teach and when to teach it?**

A: If you do not intend that your children ever attend school, you need not concern yourself about grade-level requirements. Your goal will be to give your children a rich and stimulating education. If, however, you think your child may eventually enter the school system, you may want to give some thought as to which type of school she will attend and what that school's requirements are. For example, a Montessori school, a Waldorf school, a Catholic school, and a public school have different grade-level expectations. Broad, national grade-level books, like *What Every Fourth Grader Should Know* and *Learn at Home, Grade 4* are available at local bookstores. World Book Encyclopedia also has a list of grade-level requirements available free on their Web site, www.worldbook.com/ptrc/html/curr.htm. For a list of the grade-level expectations for your local public school, contact your local homeschooling support group. (See Appendix A for more information on how to find support groups.)

Q: What is a curriculum and do I have to use it?

A: A curriculum tells you what to teach and how to teach it. Some homeschoolers like using a curriculum because they feel it keeps them on track and helps ensure that their child is covering the same materials as the schools. Other homeschoolers do not use a curriculum because they feel it restricts them too much, costs too much, and takes too much time to use. The choice is yours as to whether or not you will use a curriculum and it's not unusual for a parent to start out using one and then gradually fade it out as they build up their self-confidence and get to know their child's interests. Homeschooling allows you to choose the way that works best for your child and for your family. Always keep your child's learning style and interests in mind, and use a curriculum if it fits your needs or covers a subject your child needs to learn or has an interest in. If you have determined that your child is a visual learner, a curriculum that has a large component of audio resources won't be very effective. Be sure to do your research before you purchase, and take the time to find a curriculum that fits your child, not one that your child has to fit. A superior education is one that works with your child's intelligence and learning styles, not against them. For more information on how to determine your child's learning style and how to tailor his homeschooling to that style, see Chapter Seven.

Q: **How do I homeschool all my children at the same time?**

A: It takes a bit of juggling, but with practice you will be able to oversee all of your children's learning. But remember, your job is not so much to teach them as it is to facilitate their learning and show them how they can learn from each other and how they can educate themselves.

Q: **How will I know if my child is learning?**

A: Children are always learning—they can't help it! Children are born hungry for knowledge and exploration of their world. Homeschooling parents know their children are learning each day because they talk with them, play with them, and learn right alongside them. Homeschooling parents can look at the whole person and concentrate on what their child knows instead of what their child does not know. Some families participate in standardized tests by choice or because it is required in their state. Parents should always ask themselves the following questions before having their child tested: How might this process affect my child? How will the test results be used? Are there less intrusive alternatives that can be used? Would my child gain anything from taking this test? Many homeschooling families use portfolios (a collection of the child's work) to show what their child has accomplished. Information about testing, portfolios, and record keeping is covered in depth in Chapter Three.

Q: **Can you homeschool a gifted child or a child with special needs?**

A: Homeschooling is an excellent option for gifted and special needs students. Because homeschooling is one-on-one learning, each child is able to learn in their own way and at their own pace. This means that if your child is advanced in reading she can do work that is challenging for her, and if she is behind in math she can work at a lower level until she catches up. For special needs students this means that they can learn in a way that works best for them. For example, a blind homeschooler may learn from braille and audio books, a deaf student can learn by reading and by watching closed-caption educational shows, and a hyperactive child can do his studies while moving around the room. Remember, all children are gifted and all children have special needs. Regardless of your challenges, homeschooling allows you to honor your children's unique learning style so that you can help them develop their special gifts. More information about this topic is available in Chapter Seven.

Q: **How do I find homeschoolers in my area?**

A: The best way to connect with homeschoolers in your area is to join a local support group. Homeschool.com has an up-to-date list of support groups for the United States and for other countries. Go to www.homeschool.com/localsupport and select the name of your state or country. Appendix A also has a list of support groups by state.

Q: **How has the Internet affected homeschooling?**

A: Whether you're a child, a college student, or an adult, the Internet has turned every home into a virtual homeschool. Now adults are taking business courses online, college students are attending virtual universities, and children can follow their interests and learn about the things that matter most to them. More and more parents are homeschooling their children because of better Internet access and the increased amount of quality educational materials available online. People who only a few years ago would never have dreamed of homeschooling their kids now feel confident to do so because of the Internet. The Internet has been especially beneficial for older students, since online programs that tie into secondary school curricula make it easier for children to be homeschooled during their high school years. Homeschooling and online learning are a powerful combination because the two together allow children the flexibility to pursue their interest in a subject to a Ph.D. level if they choose rather than being stopped at the eighth grade level because of their age. The Internet also allows students to interact and work with students of different cultures, races, nationalities, and religious traditions. In the fast-moving information age, children can learn about anything they are interested in at any time via the Internet—they just have to know where to look. When you know where to look, the Internet can help you build an education for your child that is customized and individualized to meet his interests and skills. Chapter Nine explores some of the best educational resources available on the Internet.

Q: **How do I tell my relatives and friends that we've decided to homeschool?**

A: Dropping the bomb and telling your friends and relatives that you have decided to homeschool can be very difficult. It's not easy being "different," especially when you are exploring something for the first time and are not completely sure of yourself yet. Although homeschooling is considered to be a mainstream option in education today, many relatives still react negatively when you tell them of your decision. After all, they sent their children to school and most likely their children turned out just fine. Diplomacy and tact can be a big help in this situation. If your friend or relative is worried that your child may not receive a good education, you can show them some of the academic statistics in this book and tell them about some of the famous people who were homeschooled as children. If your relatives are worried about socialization, you can tell them about the activities your children are going to participate in. Sometimes, a friend or relative may respond with anger or envy that you get to be with your children all the time and they do not. It's important for homeschoolers and nonhomeschoolers to remember that life is full of choices. You do the best you can and try to make the decisions that are right for your family. We are fortunate as a society just to have so many educational options. Whether your child attends a private school, a public school, or a homeschool, the important thing is not to do what is right for your neighbor or your relative but to do what is right for you and your children. As your homeschooling journey progresses and it becomes more and more obvious that your children are doing well academically and socially, some of those who were the most negative at first will become your biggest supporters.

Q: What if my spouse doesn't want to homeschool, but I do?

A: Homeschooling is a radical idea for some people, and your spouse may need a little time to get used to the idea. It will help if you can show your spouse how well homeschoolers are doing academically and socially. Read some of the books listed in the Homeschooling Resource Guide at the end of this book and discuss some of the more interesting points with your partner. If your spouse still has some reservations, you might suggest a one-year trial period. Homeschooling is not something everyone does and it can be scary to be different. A trial period will take some of the pressure off and will give you a chance to see how homeschooling will work for your family.

Q: How can I get my child excited about homeschooling (especially if they have been in school for sometime)?

A: In order for homeschooling to work your child must become a full partner in her education. First, you must put your child's fears to rest by reassuring her that if she homeschools she will still be able to see her friends. In fact, because homeschooling takes less time than classroom learning, she will probably have more time for her friends. Plus, she will have extra time to pursue her interests and her hobbies. If your child is older, encourage her to read the book *The Teenage Liberation Handbook*. This book will remind her just how powerful she is and will encourage her to take charge of her own learning. Be honest with your child and explain to her why you think homeschooling is a good idea. If she is still reluctant, you can suggest a one-year trial period. If, after a year, homeschooling doesn't work for her, she can always return to school. But this time she'll be in school because she *wants* to be there—and that will make all the difference.

Q: How can homeschooling benefit the religious family?

A: By law, public schools must maintain a separation of church and state and therefore cannot include religious or moral training in their curriculum. Homeschools have no such restriction and therefore you can weave your family's spiritual beliefs into your child's studies. For example, Christian families may use a

Christian curriculum for science and other subjects and Muslim and Jewish homeschoolers may organize their homeschooling around daily devotionals. One of the benefits of homeschooling is that you can pass your personal beliefs on to your children and can help them develop morals and values that will serve them later in life.

Q: Can I homeschool if I'm a single parent?

A: Yes, you can homeschool your children if you are a single parent but you will probably need to adjust your work schedule. Fortunately, the work environment is changing and single-parent homeschoolers can take advantage of flex time, telecommuting, and part-time work to help them get the income they need. It also helps to have a strong network of family and friends. More information on work and homeschooling is available in Chapter Eight.

Q: Can I homeschool if I'm overseas?

A: Homeschooling is growing in popularity around the world, particularly in Australia, New Zealand, South Africa, the United Kingdom, and Japan. Still, homeschooling originated in the United States, and because of that there are more homeschooling resources and opportunities available in America than anywhere else. If you are an American living overseas, you can use an American independent study program to help you while you are away. If you plan on living overseas for an extended period of time and your child is in high school, you may want to consider participating in the international baccalaureate program, which gives your child an international diploma that he can use for admittance to some of the finest universities in the world. If you are serving in the military overseas, the Military Homeschool Network (www.militaryhomeschool.com) has information on how to get started.

HOMESCHOOLING IS NOT NEW . . .

- George Washington
- John Quincy Adams
- Abraham Lincoln
- Theodore Roosevelt
- Benjamin Franklin
- John James Audubon
- Alexander Graham Bell
- Wilbur and Orville Wright
- Robert Frost
- Wolfgang Amadeus Mozart
- General Douglas MacArthur
- Florence Nightingale
- Agatha Christie

all were either taught at home or taught themselves!

Q: **How do I get started?**

A: Most homeschooling adults begin their journey by first reading everything that is available about homeschooling, attending a homeschooling conference, and/or joining a local homeschooling support group. Chapter Three is all about getting started and has recommendations on what to read, how to set educational goals for your child, how to select your learning materials, how to comply with legal requirements, and how to organize your home to make it "learning friendly." So keep reading and you'll feel like a homeschooling expert in no time.

IS HOMESCHOOLING RIGHT FOR YOU?

Homeschooling is not as difficult as you might imagine, but it does require a strong commitment by you and your child. You probably already have a good idea as to what type of education you want for your child and you'll soon know if homeschooling is what you've been looking for. One very important aspect to consider is the amount of time you'll be spending with your children. So before you decide to homeschool, you'd better make sure that you like spending lots of time with your kids!

There are also financial implications for most families, since one parent must stay home with the children, at least part-time. At a time when it can take two incomes just to get by, living on one income can cause financial problems and stress for some families. Whether you decide to homeschool or not, the most important thing is to find the educational setting that is right for your child. Should you decide to homeschool, remember that you are not alone. There is plenty of help available: tutors, team teaching, distance learning courses, support groups, co-ops, Web sites, and more!

"WHY DID YOU DECIDE TO HOMESCHOOL?"

"I began homeschooling because my daughter's kindergarten teacher told me that my daughter could not learn! My daughter was bored and didn't know what to do. She was reading at a third grade level, when her classmates were still learning their ABCs."

Joan

"I remembered how much of my time was wasted in school waiting in lines, waiting on the other kids to settle down and receive instruction, and because of my frustration at being held to the pace of the group. Later, it became more important to me that my daughter be treated as I wanted her treated, and that she not spend so much time in the company of children whose habits I might not approve of."

Trish—Pensacola, Florida

"We decided to homeschool after two frustrating years of trying to get the public school to give my son extra reading help. They said yes, he had a reading comprehension problem, but since he was big in size they didn't want to label him and so they continued to pass him even though he wasn't reading. When they finally did approve him for help, the class was so big, there was no way this was going to make a difference. So I thought, 'I can do this myself.'"

Tammy

"My son had been in a gifted and fast-paced curriculum for the first three years of his education. Suddenly it became politically incorrect to separate out gifted children and give them the education they needed, just as you would a child with a learning disability, and the class was split up and tossed in with the regular-pace children, who had ended the previous school year four months behind my son's class in the grade curriculum. The gifted children were bored and became the 'problem' children in the two classes they had been split up into. After two and a half months of trying to make the school keep its word that the gifted children would continue to receive the accelerated studies they needed to maintain their interest, most of the parents of the gifted children decided to pull their children from the school and sent them to charter schools or homeschool."

Julia—Battle Creek, Michigan

"My journey into homeschooling started with becoming a special education teacher during the years before my children were born. Teaching children with learning disabilities taught me the importance of an individualized education. Every child is so unique with varied gifts, talents, and abilities. Discovering the gifts in each child, then encouraging those gifts, is an extremely important part of my job, and my homeschooling."

Terra—Austin, Texas

"I decided to homeschool my child when his grades dropped 11 points in a six-week period and his public-school teacher didn't think that indicated a problem since it was still a B-. I gave the situation another six-week period and his grades continued to drop. The teacher indicated to me that he was still passing and had to fail in order to receive help, such as tutoring or remedial teaching. I requested that homework or school classroom work be sent home so that I could reteach the day's lesson and was told that the school did not believe in parents teaching their children. The teacher had decided that my son was lazy. My son had developed a lot of internal anger; his self-esteem was very low and he hated school. We looked into private schools, but I was afraid that we would just be transferring a problem. Homeschooling looked like a very good solution. My son liked the idea and we began after winter break. The last day before vacation I went to the school with my son to get all of his personal belongings. As we left the building, he asked if he ever had to come back, and I told him no. I could actually see the weight drop off his shoulders and his step become lighter. I knew then that no matter what happened, we had made the right decision to homeschool."

Kathy—Plano, Texas

"We began homeschooling three years ago, immediately following the shootings in Columbine. My husband and I had had our fill of school violence. The constant worry (for two working parents) was more than we could take. My children are very intelligent, yet they were struggling in the public school system and were always unhappy. I realize that we cannot protect our children from harm's way for their entire life, but we could make a conscious decision to protect them while in school, *and* provide the type of education they deserve and we expected. We gave our children the choice of private school or homeschool. Unanimously, they voted for homeschooling. I laugh when I remember their decision, because I think they were thinking, 'This will be so much easier!' But they did not realize that I am tougher on them than any public-school teacher had been!"

Patricia—Popular Grove, Illinois

"When it came time for my daughter to go to traditional kindergarten, I just felt that there was no reason to be sending her away for the day, away from us, away from our daily activities, away from our daily discussions, to the charge of basically unfamiliar adults. It did not feel right. Over the years I have realized even more deeply how the time I spend with my children now will ultimately benefit them later. I am the one who knows them better than anyone. I am the one who can nurture their interests and hopefully continue to keep that spark of curiosity and desire to learn alive and well."

Theresa—Eleva, Wisconsin

CHAPTER THREE

Getting Started: The First Year

THE NUMBER-ONE QUESTION THOUSANDS of parents ask is probably your next question: How do I get started? The good news is that it is not hard to get started homeschooling, and certainly not as hard as many parents perceive it to be. Although there are some legal issues to be dealt with, you will find you don't have to: fill out forms as complex as your tax return, declare to the world and (yikes) Aunt Mildred that you are now homeschooling your children, join a group of perfect homeschooling parents (there are no perfect homeschooling parents), or add a costly addition to your home for a classroom.

Before you pull your children out of school or send them to school for the first time, examine what would be your best starting point, given your family's unique lifestyle and needs. Have your children been in school and need to rekindle their interest in learning? Do you need to rearrange your work hours? Can your high-school-age homeschooler do most of his homeschooling himself? Do you have a special needs child and need additional assistance developing an educational plan for her? The reason homeschooling works so well is that it can be customized to fit your family's needs, financial situation, living environment, parents' work hours, and child's educational needs and interests. Perhaps, because of a home business, you and your spouse are available mostly in the late afternoon and early evening to work with your children. Maybe your children learn with their grandmother during the day while you are at work and you tackle great family educational endeavors at night and on the weekends. Remember, homeschooling (because it is individualized) does not take as much time as classroom learning. Perhaps either you or your spouse has decided to quit working and stay home full-time to homeschool your children. The Emery family from Lynnwood, Washington, is not only a homeschooling family, they are also an RV-schooling family. The Emerys don't even have a traditional "home," since they are traveling through America in an RV and using the real world as their classroom and home. Just as no family situation is the same, your homeschool does not have to be the media version of homeschooling (alert, perfect kids sitting at the kitchen table with Mom teaching). You can choose to set up a highly organized and scheduled homeschool (where your children learn certain subjects at certain times), or you may prefer an unstructured approach (where they learn according to their own rhythms). Since your children's needs and interests change over time, you may find that the style of homeschooling you start out with is not the style of homeschooling you end up with. The goal is to set up an educational plan that makes sense for your family and work schedules, and one that also focuses on your child's individual goals and learning style. The remainder of this chapter discusses in detail the following steps you can take to get your homeschool off to a good start:

- Begin with a homeschooling "exploration" period
- Become homeschooling savvy
- Learn about the different homeschooling styles
- Set your goals
- Choose curriculum and other learning materials
- Get organized
- Evaluate your child's progress
- RELAX and enjoy this special time with your children

"IF I'D ONLY KNOWN_____WHEN I WAS GETTING STARTED."

"If I only knew how much support and help there was out there when we began homeschooling. When my children were evaluated recently, they were asked what they liked most about homeschooling. The answers were 'being home with Mom all day' and 'learning.' I think so many children want to be closer to their parents, but work schedules and extra activities don't allow this and it's a shame."

Tammy

"If I only knew that homeschooling is the scientific method at work. You simply try different things to find out what works. If your child seems to be happily engaged in an activity—then what you are doing is working. If your child pouts, cries, and resists—then what you are doing isn't working. Be willing to get rid of what doesn't work, and move on to something that does. Learning should be a joyful experience even though it may be very messy, confusing, and hectic. My best advice is to embrace the chaos."

Diane Keith—editor, *Homefires: A Journal of Homeschooling*

"I wish I had known that it is better not to decide on a curriculum before you know your child's learning style, strengths, interests, etc. I have a number of books and a year's math curriculum gathering dust."

Trish—Pensacola, Florida

"If I had known homeschooling was legal before they started public school, they never would have gone. I wasn't aware of any of the laws or where to begin. It has been absolutely wonderful. I don't have to worry about my kids anymore. At their school they had bomb scares, kids bringing butcher knives to kindergarten, etc. It was horrible. People are not happy with the public school system at all, they just aren't sure of the other options!"

Lisa—Elkland, Missouri

"If we'd only known what a transition it would be when we began homeschooling. We all had to adapt to 'this is Mommy/discipline time' vs. 'this is teacher-giving-you-space-to-learn time.' We also had to adapt to the change it made to the household. We needed to give them more opportunity to make messes in the house for the sake of learning, instead of trying to keep the house in a particular kind of order."

Max and Amy—Culver City, California

"My piece of advice for new people out there: If you're going to pull your children out of public school, don't do so unless you 'know the cost' and are committed to do it for the entire school year. I see so much damage and time lost for the kids whose parents wanted to do homeschooling for the novelty of it. Then half a year later saying, 'Oh, I just can't do it. I didn't know how hard it was going to be. I want my own time back!'"

Maria—Deer Trail, Colorado

"Between church events, karate classes, homeschool P.E. class, group field trips, and going to friends' houses, socialization is not a problem. He is with other children at some point every day of the week. It really bugs me, because I know there are schools in our area where the children are not allowed to talk in the classroom, the hall, or the cafeteria. It wouldn't be so bad except they get recess only two times a day (and that is dependent on the weather). People should be worried about the socialization issues in the school instead of worrying about homeschoolers socializing!"

Janet—Harahan, Louisiana

"If I'd only known more people who homeschooled when we began. The one family I knew was very rigid with their schedule and that just didn't work for us. As I branched out and joined our local support group, I was introduced to other ways of homeschooling. I have read many books and visited many sites on the Internet. I am constantly wanting to hear stories from others because it usually gets me thinking about ways I can improve our experience."

Trisha—Elkhart, Indiana

START WITH A HOMESCHOOLING "EXPLORATION" PERIOD

After you have done your research and decided to homeschool but before you purchase supplies and begin formal homeschooling, set aside six months as an exploration period. This exploration period will allow you and your children to get to know each other better, which is especially important if your children have been in school, and will give your children a chance to get to know themselves better. Financially, this exploration period will save you from spending money on materials you might not really need or use. Instead, you'll use this time to collect educational catalogues and circle the items you think you might want. But don't buy anything yet! After a few months of spending time with your children, you'll have a better idea what their interests are and how they learn best.

Use this exploration period to get to know your community better. Now that you have the time, you and your children can explore museums, take hikes, and put together your own field trips. You'll also have a chance for more reading; you'll be able to read those homeschooling books and magazines you've heard so much about, and your children will be able to read books of their own choosing. This is a rare treat for children who are used to having a teacher tell them what to read. Your children will also have time to make new friends and develop new hobbies.

Some parents like the idea of taking an exploration period, but worry that their children will fall behind. They won't. You are not taking time off from learning, you are building a strong foundation for learning—a foundation based on an intimate knowledge of your children and what works best for them. And you will begin your more formal studies knowing that your children are well rested—physically, emotionally, and spiritually. Your children may never have another opportunity like this. Give yourselves this special time to rekindle your passion for life and learning. You will be creating memories that will last a lifetime.

Post the following in a prominent spot in your home during your first year homeschooling:

HOMESCHOOLING "DOUBT BUSTERS"

- There are no picture-perfect homeschooling families. There are no picture-perfect homeschooling children, and you are not a picture-perfect parent. There is no such person, so don't try to be one. (The "supermom" syndrome is dead. Good riddance.)
- Can any teacher be as committed to your child's success as you?
- You don't have to have a lot of money, a full-time maid (although once-a-week help is nice), a teaching credential, or the patience of Mother Teresa to homeschool your children successfully.
- Your mother-in-law and other family members will come around. You may be pleasantly surprised that the person in your family who objected the most to your homeschooling your kids can become your biggest supporter.

- The government is not going to show up at your doorstep and take your kids away if you homeschool them. Just handle the legal issues pertinent to your state and school district when applicable, and relax.
- The one-on-one attention your child receives at home, even if it is one hour a day, two hours a day, or minutes weaved together throughout the day, far exceeds what he would ever learn in a classroom in a given day.
- Even if you and your child access tutors, online curricula, and community classes for her homeschool education, you will have a good feel for what she is learning. She will share it with you or you will be right there at her side as she learns. You won't miss a major hole in her education.
- Homeschoolers have made it! Children who have never stepped foot in a traditional classroom are out in the world, right now, as adults, living successful, fulfilled, purposeful, and, in many cases, extraordinary lives! Homeschooling works.

BECOME A HOMESCHOOLING EXPERT

As a new homeschooler, one of the first steps you should take is to learn about the law in your state. Homeschooling is legal throughout the United States, but the requirements are different in each state. Some states require homeschoolers to be tested each year. Some states require that you sign up as if you were a private school. Some simply ask you to file a notice of intent to homeschool. The National Home Education Network (NHEN) has put together a list of each state's homeschooling laws. (See Appendix B.)

Some homeschoolers do not have to comply with state homeschooling laws because they join independent study programs (ISPs). ISPs file attendance forms and academic records for the student and in some cases even issue diplomas. ISPs may be an extension of the local public school or a separate private company. For example,

Clonlara Day School in Ann Arbor, Michigan, has an extended homeschooling program, where children from over twenty-five countries homeschool in many different ways and still receive a private-school diploma. A list of independent study programs and distance private schools is available in the Homeschooling Resource Guide.

When Rebecca first learned about homeschooling, she called the California Department of Education and was told that homeschooling was illegal. Of course, that is not true, but the school system loses average daily attendance moneys when parents pull their children out of school, so it is not in the Education Department's best interest to help you with your homeschooling.

The best way to learn about ISPs, charter schools, and the laws in your area is to contact your local homeschooling support group. The contact information for these groups changes often, so Homeschool.com has created a special "local support" section, where support groups post their own updates about conferences, laws, contact information, etc. This list is available at www.Homeschool.com/localsupport.

TOP TEN BOOKS ABOUT HOMESCHOOLING

1) *Homeschooling for Excellence* by David and Micki Colfax

2) *The Teenage Liberation Handbook: How to Quit School and Get a Real Life and Education* by Grace Llewellyn

3) *Dumbing Us Down: The Hidden Curriculum of Compulsory Schooling* by John Taylor Gatto

4) *The Unschooling Handbook: How to Use the Whole World as Your Child's Classroom* by Mary Griffith

5) *The Homeschooling Book of Answers: The 88 Most Important Questions Answered by Homeschooling's Most Respected Voices* edited by Linda Dobson

6) *Deschooling Our Lives* edited by Matt Hern

7) *The Successful Homeschool Family Handbook: A Creative and Stress-Free Approach to Homeschooling* by Raymond and Dorothy Moore

8) *The Well-Trained Mind: A Guide to Classical Education at Home* by Jessie Wise and Susan Wise Bauer

9) *The Homeschooling Handbook*, 2nd Edition by Mary Griffith

10) *Homeschoolers' Success Stories: 15 Adults and 12 Young People Share the Impact That Homeschooling Has Made on Their Lives* by Linda Dobson

When you first make the leap and decide to homeschool, you feel daring, powerful, and incredibly free. Unfortunately, there are also moments when you feel a bit panicky and wonder how you ever had the audacity to make such a move. Reading books and articles about homeschooling will quiet your fears and build up your self-confidence. About.com (www.homeschooling.about.com) and A to Z Home's Cool (www.gomilpitas.com/homeschooling/index.htm) both offer rich selections of articles about all aspects of homeschooling, everything from "Dropping the Bomb: Telling Friends and Relatives You've Decided to Homeschool" to "Is Your Child Gifted?" Books about homeschooling are also very helpful. The major chain bookstores, particularly Barnes & Noble, Borders, and Amazon.com, carry a wide selection of homeschooling books, and these books can turn you into a homeschooling expert in no time!

TOP HOMESCHOOLING WEB SITES

Homeschool.com (www.Homeschool.com)

- the number-one homeschooling site on the Internet, according to *Forbes* magazine (2000)

- e-newsletter featuring exclusive interviews and original articles on broad homeschooling topics
- official homeschooling gateway for the JASON Project, and ChildU online curriculum
- personal advisers for each homeschooling style

About.com (www.homeschooling.about.com)

- articles, lesson plans, and unit studies for weekly homeschooling support
- e-newsletter filled with practical suggestions and lesson plans
- unit studies for every state in the United States and province in Canada

A to Z Home's Cool (www.gomilpitas.com/homeschooling/index.htm)

- great searchable archive of homeschooling articles

HOMESCHOOLING STYLES

Although every homeschool is unique, certain homeschooling "styles" have become very popular. Most homeschoolers do not follow one style or method exactly. Instead, they select the ideas and suggestions that fit their family and eventually end up with a method all their own. It may take some time to develop your own routine and you may discover that you start out more structured in the beginning and become more flexible and relaxed as time goes on. The following are the most popular homeschooling styles. The sample schedules presented are geared for younger children.

School-at-Home

School-at-home is the style most often portrayed in the media because it is so easy to understand and can be accompanied by a photo of children studying around the kitchen table. This is also the most expensive method and the style with the highest burnout rate. Most families who follow the school-at-home approach purchase boxed curricula that comes with textbooks, study schedules, grades, and record keeping.

TYPICAL SCHOOL-AT-HOME SCHEDULE

The school-at-home family follows the schedule established by the curriculum they purchased. For example:

8–9:00 a.m. Children dress, tidy house, and have breakfast.

9–10:00 a.m. Reading (using spelling books, writing assignments, and free reading)

10–10:30 a.m. Math (using a textbook and workbook)

10:30–11:00 a.m. History on Monday/Wednesday (using a textbook)

Science on Tuesday (using a textbook that includes occasional experiments)

Geography on Thursday (using a workbook)

11–noon. Electives (usually a foreign language audio program, an art course, or another elective that was included in the curriculum)

For help, school-at-home families contact their curriculum provider. Their children may also turn assignments in to the curriculum provider for grading and evaluation.

Some families use the school-at-home approach but make up their own lesson plans and find their own learning materials. The advantage of this style is that families know exactly what to teach and when to teach it. That can be a comfort when you are just starting out. The disadvantage is that this method requires much more work on the part of the teacher/parent and the lessons are not as much fun for the children. A complete list of curriculum suppliers is available in the Homeschooling Resource Guide.

Unit Studies

Unit studies use your child's interest in a subject and then tie that subject in to subject areas like math, reading, spelling, science, art, and history. For example, if you have a child who is interested in ancient Egypt, you would: learn the history of Egypt, read books about Egypt, write stories about Egypt, do art projects about pyramids, and learn about Egyptian artifacts or mapping skills to map out a catacomb.

TYPICAL UNIT STUDIES SCHEDULE

Unit studies can refer to a relaxed, interest-led exploration through a subject, or a traditional approach, using packaged unit studies. Although most unit studies will be done at home, some families do get together to work on the larger units.

Monday: Get together with the other families who will be participating in a Little House unit study and assign responsibilities, such as sewing, food, reading material, and so on.

Tuesday: As a group, learn about pioneer clothing and make, rent, or buy a pioneer outfit to wear the rest of the week.

Wednesday: As a group, learn about pioneer cooking and food storage. Make recipes from the *Little House Cookbook*, including grinding wheat and making butter.

Thursday: Individually, research and write about the life of Laura Ingalls Wilder.

Friday: As a group, sew a friendship quilt that will be sent to a needy homeschooling family.

For help, the unit studies family would turn to the Internet for ideas and research, to unit study lesson providers for packaged lessons, and to other homeschooling families for ideas and participation.

Packaged unit studies are available on popular topics like the Little House and American Girl books and also for virtues like patience, trust, and obedience. The advantage of this homeschooling method is that it recognizes the fact that people learn best when they are interested in the topic. The disadvantage is that sometimes parents can be overzealous and make a unit study out of everything, scaring the child off from talking about a new interest they might have. Free unit studies are available from www.unitstudies.com and from Unit Study Adventures at www.unitstudy.com. Some families also start their own "scout school" and use www.meritbadge.com to supplement their curriculum. Information about Scout School is available at www.geocities.com/cherokeegs/scoutschool.

"Relaxed," or "Eclectic" Homeschooling

"Relaxed" or "Eclectic" homeschooling is the method used most often by homeschoolers. Basically, eclectic homeschoolers use a little of this and a little of that, using workbooks for math, reading, and spelling, and taking an unschooling approach for the other subjects.

TYPICAL RELAXED/ECLECTIC HOMESCHOOLING SCHEDULE

For the family who practices "relaxed," or "eclectic," homeschooling, mornings are often used for more formal, "have to" work, and afternoons are used for hobbies and other special projects.

There are no specific times set up for each subject, but instead the child is expected to meet their educational goals.

Reading: Read one chapter a day from a book the child has chosen. The parent will also often read challenging books to the children at night, like *Jane Eyre, Phantom of the Opera, The Three Musketeers,* and other classics.

Writing: Eclectic families usually center their writing around journals, essays, letters to friends, and the occasional report. Some families also participate in a "young writers" club, available through their support group.

Math: Each child will have the math materials that best suit their learning style. One child may use math software, one child may use math manipulatives like rods, shapes, and counters, another child may use a math textbook. The parent then evaluates the child's retention by periodically making up a sheet of problems that review all the math concepts the student has learned.

Science: The emphasis is on hands-on experiments that the family does at home or through community science classes (like those put on by MadScience.com).

History/Geography: The family will use workbooks, software, educational games, and historical fiction. Some families also make up time lines and history notebooks like those used in the classical and Charlotte Mason approaches.

Special Interests: Afternoons are generally spent doing special projects, pursuing hobbies, and participating in community classes and teams like soccer, gymnastics, Boy Scouts, and 4-H.

For help, the eclectic homeschooler may rely on regular classroom standards for their child's grade level (for example, studying multiplication in the second grade, California missions in the fourth grade, and United States history in the ninth grade). They may also use standardized tests to measure their child's progress.

The advantage of this method is that the parent feels that the subjects they believe are most important are covered thoroughly. This method also allows the family to choose textbooks, field trips, and classes that fit their needs and interests. A complete list of books, catalogues, and online curriculum is available in the Homeschooling Resource Guide. A good magazine for the eclectic homeschooler is *Home Education Magazine* (1-800-236-3278).

Unschooling

Unschooling is also known as natural, interest-led, and child-led learning. Unschoolers learn from everyday life experiences and do not use school schedules or formal lessons. Instead, unschooled children follow their interests and learn in much the same way as adults do—by pursuing an interest or curiosity. In the same way that children learn to walk and talk, unschooled children learn their math, science, reading, and history. John Holt, schoolteacher and founder of the unschooling movement, told educators in his book, *What Do I Do Monday?*: "We can see that there is no difference between living and learning, that living is learning, that it is impossible, and misleading, and harmful to think of them as being separate. We say to children, 'you come to school to learn.' We say to each other [educators], 'our job in school is to teach children to learn.' But the children have been learning, all the time, for all of their lives before they met us. What is more, they are very likely to be much better at learning than most of us who plan to teach them something."

TYPICAL UNSCHOOLING SCHEDULE

Every unschooler's schedule is different and will follow the interests of the child for that day.

Mornings: Children wake up when they are rested and decide for themselves what they would like to do that day. Some unschooling parents give their children a list of chores to do and suggestions for different activities for the day. Many unschooled children establish goals for themselves and work with their parents to set up a schedule that will help them achieve that goal. Each day will be different. One day, the child may be hungry to learn new spelling words, so they will do spelling first thing in the morning. On another day, the child may be excited to set up a special science experiment and may run to the kitchen first thing to begin their project. Unschooling parents have a tendency to leave educational materials out for their children to "discover"—they may leave the microscope out on the kitchen table, or a new book on the coffee table, or a new cookbook in the kitchen. They direct their children's learning by stimulating the child's interest in a particular project or subject.

Afternoons: Many unschoolers spend their afternoons out in the community—volunteering at the library, working at a part-time job, or taking private lessons. Unschoolers have a tendency to pursue their interests passionately and in depth for a time and then move on to their next interest. They also have a tendency to stay up late, engrossed in a good book.

For help, unschoolers turn to other homeschoolers and to the community. They set up classes and clubs together. They trade private lessons with other homeschoolers. They do not take tests and do not teach to state-mandated standards or schedules.

Ms. Pat Montgomery, homeschooling adviser for forty-seven years and founder of Clonlara Private Day School, defined unschooling in a speech she made to parents at a homeschooling conference in August 2001, titled "Unschooling: Catch the Spirit."

I think, first we have to define what unschooling is, because it is different things to different people. For some it is living and learning without any school at all. For others, it means not using any prepackaged materials. For others, it is letting kids do whatever they want. For me, unschooling is taking responsibility for your own learning and the learning of those around you. It's focusing on the interests of the child. It's focusing on your own interests, your own abilities. It's learning in spurts and it's goofing off—not necessarily in equal doses. And, all of it, for me, spells freedom. Freedom to learn. Freedom is never given. It is taken.

Unschoolers embrace that freedom and believe strongly that learning happens naturally and effortlessly and they trust in their child's ability to direct their own learning. Jedediah Purdy was allowed to spend his formative years learning naturally on a West Virginia farm. Much of this time was spent reading, being read to, roaming the woods, creating collections of natural objects, and receiving lectures on political economy while helping a Yale-graduate-turned-farmer neighbor put up hay. Jedediah moved on to Harvard, then to Yale Law School, where he was a student when he wrote the critically acclaimed *For Common Things: Irony, Trust, and Commitment in America Today*. It's no surprise that Jedediah sees a future of limitless possibilities, "a combination of teaching, writing, and doing public work, probably in the areas of environment and human rights," he says, pursuing his lifelong interest through the design of international standards for the environment.* The advantage to unschooling is that unschooled children have the time and research abilities to become experts in their areas of interest, just like Jedediah did. The disadvantage is

*This quote originally appeared in *Homeschoolers' Success Stories* by Linda Dobson (Prima, 2000), p. 38.

that because unschoolers do not follow the typical school schedule, they may not do as well on grade-level assessments and may have a harder time if they reenter the school system. Unschooling books are available from the John Holt Associates Bookstore (now operated by FUN-Books.com) at 1-888-FUN-7020.

The Work/Study/Service Method

The work/study/service method is a homeschooling style developed by the "grandparents of homeschooling," Raymond and Dorothy Moore. The Moores' formula for success involves the following: (1) studying from a few minutes to several hours a day, depending on the child's maturity, (2) manual work (working with one's hands), as least as much as study, and (3) home and/or community service, an hour a day or so. Students following the Moore Formula have received scholarships to some of the finest universities in the country.

TYPICAL WORK/STUDY/SERVICE SCHEDULE

The work/study/service model of homeschooling emphasizes equal amounts of mental and physical work, and service to the community.

6:00 a.m. Parents and children arise. Children may keep their bathrobe and slippers on until after breakfast.

7:00 a.m. Family time or worship, breakfast, children dress, morning chores

9:00 a.m. Individualized work in different subjects, including phonics/spelling, reading, penmanship, and math

10:30 a.m. Work/play break

11:00 a.m. Group projects like science experiments, reading theater plays, and arts and crafts

12:30 p.m. Lunch and quiet time

2:00 p.m. Home business (cottage industry), service to others, laboratory time, vigorous exercise, free time

5:30 p.m. Supper and family time

7:00 p.m. Bath, bedtime routine

8:00 p.m. Bedtime

For help, the work/study family can turn to the Moore Academy (1-360-835-5500) for advice about easy home businesses and how to incorporate manual work into the homeschool curriculum.

Classical Homeschooling

The "classical" method began in the Middle Ages and was the approach used by some of the greatest minds in history. The goal of the classical approach is to teach people how to learn for themselves. The five tools of learning, known as the Trivium, are reason, record, research, relate, and rhetoric. Younger children begin with the preparing stage, where they learn basic reading, writing, and arithmetic. The grammar stage is next, which emphasizes compositions and collections, and then the dialectic stage, where serious reading, study, and research take place.

TYPICAL "CLASSICAL" HOMESCHOOLING SCHEDULE

(For children under age ten)

5–6:30 a.m. Parents rise, children rise, showers, dressing, early morning chores

7:00 a.m. Breakfast, morning family meeting or worship

8:00 a.m. Daily chores from a predetermined list

8:30–9:30 a.m. General lessons, where children:

1) recite memory work

2) practice reading

3) practice oral narration

9:30–10:15 a.m. Mother reads aloud to all the children (child's choice)

10:15–11:30 a.m.

1) phonics instruction

2) copy work (the student will copy verbatim a written piece, like the Constitution, that is at their level)

3) history notebook and time line (For the time line the children keep a running time line where they can note names of people and events that they are currently studying. The history notebook is laid out by date, and children add information from their copy work, photos from their field trip to the Civil War reenactment, or their entry into the National History Day Competition [www.thehistorynet.com]).

11:30 a.m. Prepare lunch and straighten house

Noon. Lunch and midday chores

1:00 p.m. Naps and quiet time

2–2:45 p.m. Mother reads aloud (children may do arts and crafts at the same time). Children finish up their oral narrations.

2:45–4:30 p.m. Finish up academic work from the morning, play time, walks, field trips, library, and volunteering

4:40–5:00 p.m. Prepare supper, straighten house

5:00 p.m. Supper and evening chores

6:30 p.m. Evening family worship (optional)

7–7:45 p.m. Father reads aloud to the family

7:45–8:30 p.m. Family activities (like games)

8:30–9:00 p.m. Prepare for bed

9:00 p.m. Bedtime

For help, homeschoolers following the classical style can read books about this method, find Web sites about classical homeschooling, and possibly start a classical homeschooling support group.

All the tools come together in the rhetoric stage, where communication is the primary focus. Popular books on the classical approach include *The Well-Trained Mind: A Guide to Classical Education at Home* by Jessie Wise and Susan Wise Bauer and *Recovering the Lost Tools of Learning* by Douglas Wilson. Also available is the book *Teaching the Trivium* by Harvie and Laurie Bluedorn from Trivium Pursuit (1-309-537-3641).

The Charlotte Mason Method

The Charlotte Mason method has at its core the belief that children deserve to be respected and that they learn best from real-life situations. According to Charlotte Mason, children should be given time to play, create, and be involved in real-life situations from which they can learn. Students of the Charlotte Mason method take nature walks, visit art museums, and learn geography, history, and literature from "living books," books that make these subjects come alive.

TYPICAL CHARLOTTE MASON SCHEDULE

Homeschoolers using the Charlotte Mason method strive to keep variety in their schedules. They generally do academics in the morning and try to "rest the child's mind" by switching between easy and challenging tasks and between active and passive tasks. The Charlotte Mason method stresses the importance of spending lots of time outdoors (usually in the afternoon), and students are encouraged to keep a nature journal. They also look for the most interesting learning materials available and avoid anything boring. Fridays are reserved for field trips.

9–9:20 a.m. Math

9:20–9:40 a.m. Handwriting

9:40–10:00 a.m. History

10–11:00 a.m. Read-aloud literature

11–noon. Lunch

Noon. Drill (e.g., multiplication tables, ABCs, state capitals, any rote learning)

12:20–12:40 p.m. Science

12:40–1:00 p.m. Grammar

1–1:20 p.m. Latin or music or art appreciation or poetry or P.E.

1:20–2:00 p.m. Map work and read-aloud work by children

Afternoons are spent outdoors, enjoying nature.

For help, homeschoolers using the Charlotte Mason method can gather information from books, Web sites, and perhaps even create their own Charlotte Mason support group.

Students also show what they know, not by taking tests, but via narration and discussion. Popular books on this method include *A Charlotte Mason Education* and *More Charlotte Mason Education,* both by Katherine Levison.

The Waldorf Method

The Waldorf method is also used in some homeschools. Waldorf education is based on the work of Rudolf Steiner and stresses the importance of educating the whole child—body, mind, and spirit. In the early grades there is an emphasis on arts and crafts, music and movement, and nature. Older children are taught to develop self-awareness and how to reason things out for themselves. Children in a Waldorf homeschool do not use standard textbooks; instead, the children create their own books. The Waldorf method also discourages the use of television and computers because they believe computers are bad for the child's health and creativity (this idea is discussed more thoroughly in Chapter Four).

TYPICAL WALDORF HOMESCHOOL SCHEDULE

Rhythm and consistency are very important to Waldorf homeschoolers, so the daily schedule is designed to flow easily and to give the homeschooling parent plenty of time for their many responsibilities. (This is a sample schedule for a younger child.)

Circle: The day starts with a 15-minute circle. (Circle time takes place in a special spot in the house. The family lights a candle and says the morning verse. They then sing a movement verse, which usually involves finger play, a closing verse or song, and then blow out the candle.)

Main lesson: The family spends 45 minutes of focused time on reading and writing. (The family obtains lessons from a Waldorf curriculum supplier.)

Free time: During this time, the parents attend to their normal responsibilities, like household management or perhaps even running a home business, and the child watches and eventually imitates the parents' actions. In addition, parents provide opportunities for creative play (like puppets, art, or building projects).

Lunch: Children help with the preparation and cleanup.

Afternoon lesson: Science is done twice a week and math is done three times a week.

Science lessons involve frequent outings. Reading lessons are also done during this time, reading from a Waldorf reader for approximately fifteen minutes a day. This afternoon session lasts approximately one hour.

Free play: Crafts, imitation activities, and creative play occupy the child until dinnertime.

Dinner: Children help with preparation and cleanup.

Bedtime ritual: This usually takes one hour. The parent either reads aloud or tells a bedtime story.

Books about the Waldorf method are available from the Rudolf Steiner Bookstore (1-916-961-8727). Waldorf curriculum and support is available from Oak Meadow (1-818-704-1046).

Montessori

Montessori materials are also popular in some households. The Montessori method emphasizes "errorless learning," where the children learn at their own pace and in that way develop their full potential. The Montessori homeschool emphasizes beauty and quality and avoids things that are confusing or cluttered.

Wooden tools are preferred over plastic tools, and learning materials are kept well organized and ready to use.

TYPICAL MONTESSORI HOMESCHOOLING SCHEDULE

According to Montessori philosophy, children should be allowed as much unscheduled time as possible in order for them to learn to manage their own time. Children are also encouraged to select their own learning materials and to learn at their own pace, in the belief that children will be drawn to what they need.

Montessori families often set learning centers in their home, for example:

A "practical life" area, which promotes activities such as pouring, spooning, and food preparation, and includes child-size buckets, brooms, and mops for cleaning up.

A "sensorial" area, which includes such items as wooden blocks (that teach size comparison), different scents for smelling, and colored tablets for learning about colors.

A math area, which includes hands-on materials like number rods, sandpaper numbers, and colored beads for counting.

A language area, which includes sandpaper numbers, a movable alphabet, books, and phonics materials.

A "cultural" area for history and geography, which includes globes, map puzzles, time lines, books, and pictures about different cultures, and the Montessori "peace curriculum" (a course on conflict resolution for children).

A music area, which includes bells and a variety of rhythm and other instruments.

An art area, which includes drawing materials, prints from a variety of different artists (including the masters), and craft and sewing supplies.

For help, the Montessori homeschooling family would turn to their library for books about the Montessori method. They might also contact a Montessori school in their neighborhood for suggestions and guidance.

The Montessori method also discourages television and computers, especially for younger children. Although Montessori materials are available for high school students, most homeschoolers use the Montessori method for younger children. Books and curriculum on the Montessori method are available from American Montessori Consulting (1-562-598-2321).

Multiple Intelligences

Multiple intelligences is an idea developed by Howard Gardner and Harvard University's "project zero." The belief is that everyone is intelligent in his or her own way and that learning is easiest and most effective when it uses a person's strengths instead of their weaknesses. For example, most schools use a linguistic and logical-mathematical approach when teaching, but not everyone learns that way. Some students, the bodily kinesthetic learners for example, learn best by touching and not by listening or reading. My (Rebecca's) son is a very active hands-on learner who has a hard time sitting still to read. Although he is a good reader, he prefers to listen to audio versions of classical children's books while he draws or builds things. My (Elizabeth's) oldest daughter is the opposite. She is a voracious reader and learns best by reading and then writing essays to show what she knows. Most successful homeschoolers naturally emphasize their children's strengths and automatically tailor their teaching to match their child's learning style. Successful homeschoolers also adjust their learning environment and schedule so that it brings out their child's best.

A TYPICAL "MULTIPLE INTELLIGENCES" SCHEDULE

The goal in "multiple intelligences" homeschooling is to adapt scheduling and materials so that they bring out and work with the child's natural strengths.

Reading: One child may begin reading at age five, another child may not be ready until age seven. One child may learn best by being read to and by listening to audiotapes; another child may carry a book around all day.

Writing: One child may like to write with a pen or pencil, another child may prefer typing his work on a computer, and still another child may feel frustrated by the writing process and prefer to give oral reports of what she's learned.

Math: Some children learn well from workbooks, other children prefer using hands-on manipulatives like beads or fraction rods. Still others do math quickly and easily in their head and feel frustrated when forced to answer problems on paper.

Science: Almost all children learn science best by having plenty of hands-on experiences.

History/Geography: Children learn best by "doing," so families plan activities where the child can experience for themselves the clothing, food, and music of a particular era or culture.

Music/Sports/Arts: Families expose children to a variety of experiences, watch to see which activities spark their children's passion, and then support their children in that activity.

For help, the family using the "multiple intelligences" model should turn to books about learning styles.

Some children prefer structure and learn best when they are told what to do, others learn best on their own. Some children do their best work around the kitchen table, and others excel when they are out of doors. The goal for the homeschooling parents is to identify how, when, and what their child learns best and to adapt their teaching style to their child. More information about learning styles is in Chapter Seven.

"WHAT IS YOUR HOMESCHOOLING STYLE?"

"My daughter prefers school-at-home. I had intended to follow a more relaxed plan myself, but she likes having different subjects and lesson plans, and a part of each day devoted to 'schoolwork.'"

Trish—Pensacola, Florida

"We decided to use the classical approach in our homeschool. I believe that the classical approach is one that gives my child a complete education, one that teaches him to think and ask questions. I prefer my child be able to tell me why World War II took place, as opposed to telling me specific facts about World War II. I think this is the biggest difference between classical education and any other method or approach."

Whitney T.

"During our seven years of homeschooling we have used several approaches, including a unit study curriculum. Then we began using some of this and a little of that and doing lots of field trips, having more of an eclectic approach. For a couple of years we 'co-op' schooled with my sister-in-law and a close friend. It was a great experience. This year we're trying a few subjects in an online school, while keeping some of the workbook subjects that we've had success in. Our curriculum includes band for three of the kids at the local school, Civil Air Patrol for our oldest son, Boy Scouts for the middle son, and Girl Scouts for our daughters and myself, as well as active involvement and service with our church. We also include many field trips and activities with our local homeschool support group."

Sherri—Kalona, Iowa

"I am now in my thirteenth year of homeschooling and we are utilizing the childu.com curriculum, which is accessible from home-school.com. This provides curriculum on the computer for all the core subjects, including music, art, and technology. Our preschooler is doing the Jump Start Series book we found at Costco. Each one of these five children has a different learning capability. I have one who could not wait to learn to read. I have another who could do so independently without my help, and another who you had to sit with for every problem. One of my sons needed more time to learn to read due to his speech impairment. We also like to do unit studies. One of our units was six months in the medieval period. My kids made castles, clothes, recipes, a dinner menu, and a play, which they performed for our entire extended family at a dinner-dessert theater-type dinner. It was a blast. And last year, my middle daughter, now in high school, used the skills she learned in our unit studies and sewed costumes for the Seattle Repertory Theatre. What an honor."

Tammie—Burien, Washington

"Our personal homeschooling style has consisted of both non-traditional methods and a structured school-at-home approach. Each one of our daughters is so different from the other. The oldest is an independent visual learner who has learned to set short-term goals for herself. She wants to finish high school by age fourteen, so as parents, we lend her our full support, while still keeping a balance. She loves to work alone researching new things, so with her we use a school-at-home approach. The second child is between both styles. She is an independent audiovisual learner who welcomes guidance once in a while in her learning discoveries, so for her we use both styles to nurture her. Our youngest daughter is the opposite of both of her sisters. She is a kinesthetic learner who loves to move around. She welcomes guidance at every point of her learning experience, so with her we use the nontraditional approach, which is less structured. Having tried almost all available homeschooling methods, we've been able to find what works for each child."

Feyi—Cedar Hill, Texas

"Our homeschooling style is eclectic. We use a little bit of unschooling and a little bit of 'traditional.' We use a math textbook because he hates workbooks but for some strange reason enjoys using an old-fashioned hardback textbook. We cover language arts through reading and writing that are tied in with whatever theme unit we are covering. Science is learned through experimenting. He performs experiments, keeps a record of the results, and then reads to find out why the experiment turned out the way it did. History is more of a hobby to him than a requirement. He is eight years old and we spent the last eight months studying World War II because he was fascinated by it. We have read historical fiction books, read nonfiction books, watched old WWII movies, watched WWII documentaries, and listened to the music of the 1940s. He is also studying Spanish and piano."

Janet—Harahan, Louisiana

SETTING GOALS

The homeschooling style you use impacts the goals you set. For example, if you choose to do school-at-home, your goals will be the same as the public school's goal and you will try to complete certain lessons by a certain time. If you choose to unschool your children, then you will encourage your children to set their own goals. If you choose relaxed homeschooling, then you might set broad goals for history and science but very specific, semester-by-semester goals for math, grammar, and spelling. The most important thing is to be sure to consider your child's strengths, weaknesses, interests, and learning style when setting goals. You may also want to have a special reward or celebration when a goal is reached. For example, you can offer to take your child to a special amusement park once they have mastered their multiplication tables. Or, instead of paying your child an allowance, you can pay him for the academic jobs he completes. Your goals, like your homeschool, will be unique and will reflect your family's values and personality.

FIND YOUR FAMILY'S HOMESCHOOL STYLE

If reading all the different approaches to homeschooling is overwhelming, that is normal. You don't have to pick a style or approach today and do only that style as long as you homeschool. You don't have to ever choose one style. Many of the most respected voices in homeschooling recommend that you get to know how your child learns best before you decide what style of homeschooling to use. How does Joanne like to explore her world each day? Does Jeff need more time outside with experiments and field trips? Does David enjoy learning with audiotapes as opposed to books? Sometimes your children's style and your style do not match. Rebecca has one child who likes to structure her own day (much like Rebecca), while her other child is most productive working off a defined list of activities. One of Elizabeth's daughters likes to stay indoors and read and work (like her mother), while her other daughters like to be outdoors. Eventually, you will develop a schedule and method that suits your family's unique style. This is a learning process for you and your child that will keep evolving and changing as your children grow. Take the time to find your family's homeschool style, because you do have one, and, of course, use and adapt any of the styles and schedules listed above if they make sense to you and work for your child.

CHOOSING CURRICULUM AND OTHER LEARNING MATERIALS

During your exploration period you had a chance to discover your child's likes and dislikes, strengths and weaknesses. You now know what topics she is interested in and have a pretty good idea how she learns best. You also know what your goals are for the semester and which homeschooling style best suits your family. Now you are ready to put together your curriculum.

The curriculum you purchase or make will in large part be determined by the homeschooling style you choose. If you choose to start out with the school-at-home approach, you will probably want to purchase a complete curriculum for your child's grade level. Be sure to fit the curriculum to the child, not the child to the curriculum. You don't have to finish every book or workbook. Anything that makes you or your children cry is just not worth it. There are so many wonderful programs available that it is not necessary to stay with something that doesn't work for you. Be prepared to make mistakes. Every homeschooler does.

If you want to try the Charlotte Mason, classical, Waldorf, Montessori, unit studies, or Moore Formula methods, you simply contact their representatives and order your supplies from them. If you choose to use an unschooling or relaxed homeschooling approach, then you will read through the various catalogues and order the materials that help you accomplish your goals. And remember that curriculum isn't made up only of books—field trips, Web sites, kits, art supplies, college classes, community projects, piano lessons, and private lessons can also make up your curriculum.

Homeschooling can cost as much or as little as your budget allows. In general, buying materials individually costs less than buying complete programs.

Homeschooling conferences and curriculum fairs often include areas where homeschoolers can sell or trade used curriculum materials. And don't forget the Internet as a source for inexpensive online classes and free lesson plans.

Your homeschooling needs will change. What worked one year may not necessarily work the next. Your family's needs and interests will change, so buy just those materials that meet your present needs. And be sure to mold the curriculum to the child, not the child to the curriculum.

GETTING ORGANIZED

Now that you're homeschooling, you'll be using your home for living and for schooling. This means that keeping things organized can be a challenge. Unlike some families where the parents go off to work and the children go off to school all day, you will be using your home for living, for schooling, and, in some cases, even for working. Be prepared for books on the floor, science experiments on the table, 4-H projects in the backyard, and educational supply catalogues all over the house. Everyone has his own level of tolerance for chaos, so once again, your home organization system should reflect your own needs and values.

The home organization experts at OrganizedHome.com and About.com have the following advice for homeschooling families:

- Lower your standards. You are not competing with anyone else for homeschooling excellence or your home's appearance. Concentrate on the important things, like teaching your children and achieving your goals, and let the less important stuff go. You can't do everything and you'll never get it all done.
- Plan how you will attack household chores like cooking, cleaning, and laundry. Coming up with a schedule and writing it down makes the process easier and smoother.
- Get your children involved. Don't try to homeschool your children and run the house all by yourself. Your children have more time than you, and

you do them a disservice if you do not teach them how to take care of themselves. Older children can participate by taking care of younger siblings, teens can do the family shopping and help pay the bills, and everyone can be trained to fold their own laundry and put it away. Your home and your homeschool will run more efficiently if everyone is involved.

- Tidy up the house first, then do your studies or learning activities. Teach your children to "start the day" by making their bed, tidying the house, and taking care of their personal grooming. Then you don't have to worry about it the rest of the day.

- Get rid of junk. If you haven't used it for a while, you probably don't need it. If you don't need it anymore, hand it on to someone who will appreciate it. This applies to curriculum materials as well. If your children don't like certain workbooks or texts, sell them or give them to someone who might enjoy them more.

- Have a place for everything. Have a place for art supplies, school supplies, and books. Some homeschoolers give each child their own dishrack or box where school materials can be arranged subject by subject. Math manipulatives, vocabulary flash cards, and art projects in progress store neatly and can be put away in a breeze.

- Use hanging files to organize catalogues, attendance forms, learning records, and other paperwork.

- Use see-through plastic boxes instead of cardboard boxes to store puzzles, games, and LEGOs, so you can see exactly where things are.

- Be realistic about time. Build success into your scheduling by allowing enough time to complete assignments, chores, and errands without being rushed.

- Set up a school area. Some homeschoolers use an extra room for their classroom, some use the kitchen table. Use whatever space you have and organize your school supplies so that they are easily accessible. Set up a specific area to keep schoolbooks and other books and make sure this area has good lighting. Make sure you have a quiet area for difficult assignments, away from the noise and distractions of younger siblings.

- Schedule the 3 R's (reading, writing, and arithmetic) for when the children are freshest. Work one-on-one with the older children when the younger children are napping or when the other children are working independently or reading.
- Be flexible. Don't let your organization plan and time schedule control you—they are just guides to help you keep things moving along smoothly. Relax and enjoy yourselves.

EVALUATING YOUR CHILD'S PROGRESS

For homeschooling parents, failure is not an option. Who would want to fail their own children? That's why homeschooling parents are constantly evaluating learning materials and mentally monitoring how their students are doing. Most of your evaluations will be based on observation and reflection, and will be an everyday, ongoing process. In addition to observation, some families use diaries or journals to record work assignments for the day. Some families use very large calendars to record what their child accomplishes each day. And some families use a teacher's record-keeping book to keep track of assignments. As children grow older, they can keep their own records and write down the books they are reading, their activities, and whatever else they care to put in their journals.

Every state has its own requirements as to the type of record keeping and evaluations required by homeschoolers. Some states require testing, and some states require academic portfolios.

Testing is a controversial topic among homeschoolers. Some parents like testing because it reinforces their own observations that their child is learning and identifies any "gaps" or weaknesses that might exist. Testing is also used by some homeschoolers to keep their child at "grade level." Other homeschoolers dislike testing because they don't believe tests are accurate in the first place and they want their children to learn to evaluate themselves, not to rely on something or someone else to validate their learning. Most homeschoolers use testing if it helps them achieve a goal, like getting into college, but do not like to do yearly testing because it requires them to spend too much time studying for the test and takes time away from other interests. However, if your state requires academic testing, you have no choice but to comply.

Portfolios use photos, notes, and schoolwork to show what your child has learned, experienced, and accomplished. Portfolios can be kept for each grade or each semester. Some homeschoolers show progress by including two samples for a learning activity, one from the beginning of the semester and one from the end, so the child can see how she has improved. For example, you might include a sample of the child's handwriting and essay writing from the beginning of the semester and from the end of the semester.

Flexibility is an important element in both your evaluations and your record keeping. Whichever method you use to evaluate your child's learning, make sure that it is flexible and personal. Do not let testing and record keeping be the focus of your homeschooling. Remember, your goal—as parent and as educator—is to bring out your child's special gifts. And with that in mind, you can develop a system of record keeping and evaluation that celebrates your child's successes and chronicles his achievements.

HOMESCHOOLING MAGAZINES

- *Home Education Magazine*
  Has helpful articles covering a broad range of homeschooling styles.
  www.home-ed-magazine
  1-800-236-3278

- *Practical Homeschooling*
  Designed for conservative Christians who use the school-at-home approach.

www.home-school.com
1-800-346-6322

RELAX

Learning, in all its forms, is beautiful and unpredictable. Homeschooling gives you tremendous flexibility and time to adjust your materials and techniques as you go. Homeschooling isn't hard work, but like life, it is unpredictable. Try to remember to relax into homeschooling. If your daily homeschooling seems overwhelming or you are stressed out daily, you need to rethink your approach. If you are unhappy and not enjoying yourself, your children won't be happy or enjoy learning at home. Find a local homeschooling group and connect with a fellow homeschooling parent. Other homeschooling parents will be able to understand your concerns and unique situation. Learning to relax is very important when you first begin homeschooling, because you have not built up the confidence in yourself as a homeschooling parent. "Homeschool burnout" can happen in the first year and is more common with parents who have chosen the school-at-home approach to their homeschooling. If you are often tense while working with your kids and you feel you just can't get it all done in one day, be careful because you could be setting yourself up for a fall. Consider some quick changes if you feel you are close to burnout:

1. Take some time off. Don't worry about missing "important" learning time. What is more important than you and your children's health and happiness?

2. Remember why you decided to homeschool in the first place. It was because you wanted to enjoy your children and your life *more*.

3. Take a look at your routine. Can you make some changes that will help eliminate stress?

4. Are you going over and over certain areas with your kids? Would it help to take a less rigid approach?
5. Get some help. Look into a homeschooling co-op class, ask your spouse to take over an area of homeschooling, or find a college student who can work with the kids part-time.
6. Be creative. You can do it!

The next chapter is about homeschooling the younger child. Even if you don't have young children, you may want to read the sections about history, math, and science, since they contain unique insights that can help older children too.

CHAPTER FOUR

Homeschooling the Younger Child (Infancy to Age Twelve)

YOU MAY NOT REALIZE IT, BUT YOU'VE BEEN homeschooling your child since he was born. You did all you could do to be a loving, nurturing parent. You helped him learn how to walk, talk, feed himself, and explore his world. You naturally knew when to challenge him a bit and when to let nature take its course. You've been answering his questions since he was old enough to ask them, and helping him achieve his goals. You've taken him on long walks and trips to museums and zoos. You've helped him explore his world, with a constant eye on building his self-confidence. Teaching him to read and use numbers is not that different.

If you have a preschooler ready to enter kindergarten, the question you need to ask yourself is not "Should I homeschool?" The question to ask yourself is "Should I continue to homeschool?" If your child is older, you've probably already been taking an active part in her schooling by helping out with homework, science projects, book reports, and by volunteering in her classroom. Homeschooling is not that different, and in many cases much easier than dealing with the issues and pressures of having your child attend school.

"IF I'D ONLY KNOWN _____ WHEN HOMESCHOOLING MY YOUNG CHILD."

"If I only knew how quickly children outgrow your lap. How they become so independent and individual. Enjoy your babies, enjoy the time you have to just read a book without worrying about them leaving home soon or what college they will attend. Don't try to cram so much 'stuff'—just take it slow and enjoy them while they are young. Homeschooling gives you time with your children. Use it to really spend time with them."

Sherry—Corunna, Indiana

"If I could share advice with any new homeschooling mom, it would be no matter what you do—make time for you!!! I have learned that I need to get up earlier than the kids and have some quiet time to reflect on my personal things and read my Bible or even just sip coffee and watch the geese fly south. This time of the day is renewing and helps me to be able to be focused on the children when we get started. If I don't do this, then I feel rushed all day, and that is not good either. Being at peace with your world is essential in teaching little ones so they can see and learn patience—something the world lacks greatly."

Jen R.

"Dads, you have to be supportive and helpful too. Offer to listen to the kids read to you when you get home and show them you care and please, hug your wife and take her out on 'date nights' every other week so she can have a break from the kids too. Remember—7/24/365 is kind of tough for most women, so be prepared to help in that way and maybe you can cook dinner once a week. I know my boys love it when I cook for them. Let Mom go soak in the tub. Everyone benefits."

J.R.

BENEFITS OF HOMESCHOOLING THE YOUNGER CHILD

Homeschooling has certain advantages for young children. "Time" is the biggest advantage cited by homeschooling parents. Instead of being separated from their families at five years of age, young homeschoolers have extra time with the people they love, and strong bonds are allowed to continue and grow between parent and child and between brothers and sisters. An advantage has also been noted in hundreds of cases for "active" children whose youthful high energy can be accommodated more easily at home than in a classroom. Some parents have even been able to take their hyperactive ADHD child off Ritalin once they began learning at home. Thousands of children are slapped with the ADD label because they are unable to sit still for long periods of time to do boring work. The number of hyperactive boys who have been dosed with Ritalin has become epidemic. Isn't there an alternative to drugging our children so that they will sit still and pay attention? Allowing young children the freedom to move about as they learn is a very simple fix to a huge problem but one schools can't allow in their current setting. Homeschooling can.

Another advantage to homeschooling younger children has to do with peer pressure. Dr. Matthew James, an adviser at Homeschool.com, homeschooled his children for one hour a day for kindergarten through sixth grade. His children later attended a public high school and then went on to Stanford University. Dr. James believes that their success was largely due to the fact that his children had a solid foundation in the basics and were also spared from negative peer pressure until they were older and able to handle it. Dr. James advises parents to homeschool their children when they are young, even if they plan to participate in a traditional high school later on. This will give your children a solid start.

Children, particularly younger children, are learning machines. They learn by doing—by tasting, moving, touching, seeing, hearing, and smelling. This is their time for gathering information and making sense of the world. Homeschooling allows children to explore the world in their own way and at their own pace. They learn to read when they are ready and they have opportunities for hands-on experiences that aren't possible sitting behind a desk. It is important to remember that not all learning requires teaching; learning can and does happen naturally. Elizabeth discovered this with her first child. When her oldest daughter was six, she became fascinated with cheetahs. Through her daughter's continued interest and hunger to learn more about cheetahs, her daughter became a more proficient reader, which led her to learning about cheetah anatomy, which led to learning about a cheetah's natural habitat (geography), and then to their endangered species classification (science and ecology).

HOW DOES YOUR CHILD LEARN?

Young children naturally drift toward the activities they like and are good at. Observing your children in their day-to-day activities will help you discover their strengths. Does your child remember things better when pacing around the room? Does your child enjoy workbooks? Is your child a natural "builder"? Has your child shown a sustained interest in art or sports or reading? How does your child show what he knows? By writing, by talking, or by building things? People learn in different ways, and you may discover that your children learn differently from you and differently from each other. Experiment with different learning materials until you discover what's right for your child. Sometimes you will guess wrong and make a bad purchase. That's to be expected. Keep observing your child and you will discover who she is, what she likes, and how she learns best. This will have a tremendous benefit on all her future learning endeavors.

For those parents looking for a list of grade-by-grade expectations, the home-schooling guide at About.com has created a Web version of *World Book Encyclopedia*'s Typical Course of Study for Grades PreK–12th. A fine resource,

About.com has taken the topics suggested by *World Book* and found links to sites to help cover the material and/or master the skill. This information is available from About.com (www.homeschooling.about.com/library/blcs12.htm).

Information on how to bring out children's natural talents is explored in Chapter Seven.

READING—BETTER LATE THAN EARLY

For younger children, the emphasis is usually on building a solid foundation in reading, writing, and basic math. Where schools believe in starting formal learning as early as possible, most homeschoolers believe in delaying formal studies until the child is seven or older. This allows the child to mature physically and emotionally before she is asked to sit down and study.

Dr. Raymond and Dorothy Moore are probably the best-known advocates of the later-is-better approach. The Moores' 1975 book *Better Late Than Early* summarizes research supporting their contention that children are not psychologically ready for formal learning until age eight to ten. They suggest that waiting allows children to gain the maturity and logical skills necessary for formal work and prevents them from becoming frustrated and discouraged by attempts to handle material they are simply not yet ready to understand.

It is quite common for homeschooled children, especially those using a flexible homeschooling approach, to learn to read as young as three or to delay until age eight or nine. This may seem like a shocking idea, but boys in particular are often not ready to read until they are seven or older, and they quickly catch up to the early readers. Rebecca tried teaching her son to read at age four, but he just couldn't seem to remember the letter sounds or learn how to combine them. Rebecca read to her son an hour each night, and when he was seven years old he seemed suddenly to pick up a book and read aloud fluently. It was amazing! Rebecca's daughters, on the other hand, begged their mother to start teaching them to read at age five. Because of the individualized nature of homeschooling, late reading is not a handicap as it might be in a conventional school setting. Schools rely on text-based instruction, but "late" readers at home simply learn through other means, like watching educational TV and videos, asking questions, and observing the world around them. Also, since the child is not labeled as "slow" or put into the slow reading group, their self-confidence and self-esteem does not suffer. The child will grow into an enthusiastic reader, and thus view reading not only as a tool for obtaining knowledge or keeping up with others but as an enjoyable activity. Raising a lifelong reader is very different from just teaching a child to read. Approximately twenty million people in the United States can't read. Another estimated 40 million read at a fourth-grade level. While these are unacceptable numbers, there is another reading epidemic in this country. We're a nation of "*alliterates*," which means we know how to read but we don't read. A 1999 survey showed that only 45 percent of citizens read more than a half hour every day— that would include all reading from fiction to newspapers to work-related materials.* While the two hours of television the average American watches each day factors in here, could our nation's lack of interest in reading have something to do with the way we are taught to read in school? Is it because we force children to begin reading at age five, whether or not they are ready? Is it because we assign reading (instead of letting the child choose) and require book reports? Book reports in the second grade? Record numbers of children are forced to read before they are developmentally ready. Thus, reading continues to be an unpleasant experience for most of their school career. Unless a reading problem is involved, children learn to read when they are ready. It is developmental and not synchronized to meet an educator's timetable.

The best advice is to teach your child to read when they are ready, regardless of how young or old they may be. Reading specialists have observed that children display certain behaviors when they are ready to read. Specifically, the child:

- knows the alphabet
- likes to look through books and magazines

---

*Weeks, Linton. "The No-Book Report: Skim it and Weep." *Washington Post,* May 14, 2001; p. C01.

- knows the parts of the body
- knows his own first and last name and can pronounce it clearly
- can express herself verbally
- can repeat a sentence of six to eight words
- knows that writing carries a message
- pretends to read
- understands that reading goes from left to right
- comprehends and can answer questions about a short story
- can look at a picture and tell you a story about it
- can write his own first name

Reading experts say that there are certain things parents can do to encourage their child to become a lifelong reader:

- Read to your children—often! Even teens enjoy hearing a good book.
- Be a good role model and let your children see you reading.
- Let your children read books that are easy for them. This will make reading more fun for them and less of a chore.
- Avoid assigning or asking kids to do book reports. Instead, casually talk about the books they have read. How many books would you read if you had to write a book report after reading them?
- Keep books out around your house, in your car, and in your bathroom.
- Give books as gifts and rewards.

Allow your children to select the books they check out at the library and let them check out as many as they can carry (within library limits). Don't weed through their choices unless they are very young.

Imagine the joy of being with your child when he first learns to read. Cuddled up on your lap, your child will feel secure and loved while taking this big step. When veteran homeschoolers look back, their fondest memories are of reading to their children in front of the fireplace, reading while snuggled under the covers on a rainy day, and reading late into the night because the book was just too good to put down. Often parents believe that once their child can read on their own, they don't have to read to them anymore. Keep reading. When you read to a child, you are teaching her much more than the material covered in the book. Reading and cuddling together are the moments that connect families forever and lay the foundation for children to become lifelong readers.

READING AND WRITING RESOURCES

- *The Read-Aloud Handbook* by Jim Trelease
- *Why Johnny Can't Read: And What You Can Do About It* by Rudolf Flesch
- *Games for Reading: Playful Ways to Help Your Child Learn to Read* by Peggy Kaye
- *Games for Writing: Playful Ways to Help Your Child Learn to Write* by Peggy Kaye
- *Let's Go Learn's Homeschooling Reading Assessment*, www.home-school.com/letsgolearn

MATH + SCIENCE = TWENTY-FIRST-CENTURY SUCCESS

On September 27, 2000, John Glenn made national headlines again—this time here on earth. Glenn, former senator and astronaut and now chairman of the National Commission on Mathematics and Science Teaching in the 21st Century, presented a very alarming report to Richard Riley, secretary of education, titled "Before It's Too Late." Every parent of a school-age child needs to know the primary message of the Glenn Commission's report, which states: "America's students must improve their performance in math and science if they are to succeed in today's world."

The Glenn Commission gave four reasons why it is critical for children to have strong math and science skills if they are to succeed in the twenty-first century:

- The rapid pace of change in both the increasingly interdependent global economy and in the American workplace demands widespread mathematics- and science-related knowledge and abilities
- Our citizens need both mathematics and science for their everyday decision making
- Mathematics and science are inextricably linked to the nation's security interests
- The deeper, intrinsic values of mathematical and scientific knowledge shape and define our common life, history, and culture. Mathematics and science are primary sources of lifelong learning and the progress of our civilization.

The new global economy in which our children will work, live, and create will be very different from the present. Our children will compete for jobs, market share for their businesses, and opportunities for showcasing their artistic genius, not just with individuals and businesses in their town or city but all over the world. They will need to know how the financial marketplace affects their prosperity and future retirement, not just in the United States but the entire world. Whatever the role a child pursues in his future he must have a strong foundation in science and math to succeed in that role in a global economy. Without competency in math and science, our children's chance of achieving their future dreams will be slim. Our changing world is also going to be more dependent than ever on its future leaders, creators, and workers to solve the very complicated problems our nation will encounter. And, unfortunately, as it stands now, our school system is failing our children in math and science. The Glenn Commission calls our country's math and science programs "unacceptable" and states that America's school-age children are not "world-class learners" in math and science. Whether our public school system can completely reinvent its math and science curricula in time to prepare an entire generation of kids for life as adults remains to be seen. The good news for homeschooling parents is that you don't have to wait for the sweeping changes to occur in math and science education to create a superior education in math and science for your child. You have the freedom and the power to make these changes now. Building a strong foundation in math and science in the early years of a child's life is achievable for most parents and does not require that they have a degree in mathematics or rocket science.

SCIENCE

Children are natural scientists and explorers. Examining nature and figuring out how things "work" provide countless hours of fascination and opportunities for their scientific education. Young children spend huge amounts of time in the role of a "scientist." Unfortunately, for many, when they enter school, their wonder and excitement about science is destroyed by dry textbooks, uninspiring teachers, little hands-on experiment time, and learning facts and formulas. Although some parents new to homeschooling consider themselves ill equipped to teach science at home, if they continue to support their child's innate hunger for exploration and discovery, they will be laying a foundation for excellence in science in their child's later years. Consider the impact that Dr. Robert Ballard's parents had on his future. Before Dr. Ballard was a world-renowned scientist, discoverer of the RMS *Titanic*, explorer-in-residence for the *National Geographic*, and inspiring role model to millions of children around the world during his JASON scientific expeditions, Dr. Ballard was a little boy with a big dream. According to Dr. Ballard: "When I was about ten years old, my favorite book was *20,000 Leagues Under the Sea*, and my hero was Captain Nemo. I wanted to be an undersea explorer just like Captain Nemo. Fortunately, when I shared my dream with my parents, they did something very important—they didn't laugh. They actually encouraged me to live my dream and helped me explore how to make my dream come true. They said, 'Maybe you need to become an oceanographer if you want to become Captain Nemo.' So I became an oceanographer.

Then they said, 'Maybe you should explore becoming a naval officer,' and I became a naval officer. I used their support and suggestions of potential steps I could take as my guiding principles to help me reach my dream, and those principles allowed me to go on and live my dream." Dr. Ballard's parents not only encouraged their son to live his dream, they gave the world a modern-day Captain Nemo.

Homeschooling parents can access community mentors, college classes, the Internet, and science clubs, as well as a wide array of other excellent resources that will keep the natural-born scientist alive in their children.

SCIENCE RESOURCES

- *Super Science Concoctions: 50 Mysterious Mixtures for Fabulous Fun* by Jill Frankel Houser
- *Gee Whiz* by Marilyn Burns
- Mad Science (Educational and Entertaining Science Classes), 1-514-344-4181
- "All Inclusive Microscope Kit for Elementary Students" Catalogue #46729-00, Science Kit & Boreal Laboratories, 1-800-828-7777
- JASON At-Home www.homeschool.com/jason

MATH

Unfortunately, math is the one area where homeschoolers are not doing that much better than their schooled peers. In an interview in May 2001 Homeschool.com interview, Dr. William Bennett, former secretary of education, said: "Mathematics is an area where homeschoolers aren't knocking the ball out of the park." The importance of "knocking the ball out of the park" or achieving above average test scores pale in comparison to the most important reason children must master math—their future success in college, business, and the daily business of living. And again, like science, math is an area that oftentimes makes new homeschooling parents feel ill equipped to help their children learn at home. For many parents, even the word "math" brings back memories of long, tormented years in math classes so strongly, they can almost smell the musty textbooks and No. 2 pencils.

How, then, do you get past your own nightmarish math memories and help your children develop a solid foundation in math? Theoni Pappas, author of *Fractals, Googles and Other Mathematical Tales,* takes an approach to math that emphasizes the beauty and hidden wonders of mathematics. Instead of focusing solely on numbers, she attempts to open children's eyes to the incredible mathematical patterns that appear naturally in the world. In an August 2000 Homeschool.com interview she suggested five ways parents can provide a strong foundation for math at home:

1. **Don't let your fear of math come across to your kids.** Parents must be careful not to perpetuate the mathematical myth that math is only for specially talented "math types." Strive not to make comments like "They don't like math" or "I have never been good at math." When children overhear comments like these from their primary role models, they begin to dread math before even considering a chance of experiencing its wonders. It is important to encourage your children to read and explore the rich world of mathematics, and to practice mathematics without imparting negative biases.

2. **Don't immediately associate math with computation (counting).** It is very important to realize that math is not just numbers and computations but a realm of exciting ideas that touch every part of our lives—from making a telephone call to how the hair grows on someone's head. Take your children outside and point out real objects that display math concepts. For example, show them the symmetry of a leaf or angles on a building. Take a close look at the spirals in a spiderweb or intricate patterns of a snowflake.

3. **Help your child understand why math is important.** Math improves problem solving, increases competency, and is applicable in a variety of

ways. It's the same as reading. You can learn the basics of reading without ever enjoying a novel. But where's the excitement in that? With math, you could stop with the basics, but why, when there is so much more to be gained by a fuller understanding? Life is a lot more enriching when we go beyond the basics. The book *Fractals, Googles and Other Mathematical Tales* is easy to read and can help you stretch your children's minds to become involved in mathematics in ways that will not only be practical but also enhance their lives.

4. **Make math as "hands on" as possible.** Mathematicians *participate* in mathematics. To really experience math, encourage your child to dig in and tackle problems in creative ways. Help her learn how to manipulate numbers using concrete references she understands as well as things she can see or touch. Look for patterns everywhere, explore shapes and symmetries. How many octagons do you see each day on the way to the grocery store? Play math puzzles and games and then encourage your child to try to invent her own.

5. **Find funny and challenging math riddle books and read them with your child.** Help your child explore the basics of math. Help him see how math is applicable to his daily life. Not all children need to learn calculus or how to solve differential equations for their future career path, so don't worry about that now. Just help him build a strong foundation in math basics and rest assured he will be able to attain the knowledge of higher math if it is needed in his future.

MATH RESOURCES

- *Fractals, Googles and Other Mathematical Tales* by Theoni Pappas
- *Mathematical Scandals* by Theoni Pappas
- Cash Flow and Cash Flow for Kids, two family board games created by Robert Kiyosaki

HISTORY: THE TRUTH AND NOTHING BUT THE TRUTH

Young children want to learn history. They are fascinated about dinosaurs and the gold rush—they are fascinated about their parents' childhood. "Tell me what it was like when you were a kid, Dad." Learning history is important for children because it helps them make sense of their world. History helps answer questions like "Who is this on my quarter and on my dollar bill? Why is he important?"

Without history there is no cause and effect between events, inventions, or artistic creations. History explains *why* Columbus sailed to America, *why* Michelangelo painted the Sistine Chapel's ceiling, and *why* Americans fought the Civil War. History is not separate from science or mathematics or music or poetry. History ties them all together in a way that helps children make sense of the past and the present.

Homeschoolers are at an advantage when it comes to learning history because families can use "original source" materials like biographies and official documents to learn about events and people. Unlike schooled children, who must often rush through material in order to complete state requirements, homeschooled children can delve into the past and learn about an event until they are completely satisfied. Homeschoolers are also at an advantage when it comes to learning history because they can learn it in any way they choose. They can learn about history in a chronological order, from past to present, or they can learn about history in a way that supports their interests. For example, a girl might want to learn about all the famous women in history, or a science lover might want to learn about famous inventors and how one invention affected another.

Most parents would agree that learning history is important, yet parents believe they are bad at history. They can't remember important dates and, just like children who study history in school, they tend to think of history as boring and irrelevant. The fact that most Americans can't answer basic history questions is an interesting phenomenon. Joy Hakim and James Loewen believe they know why. (Joy Hakim is the author of *A History of Us,* an eleven-volume history series that is very popular with homeschoolers. James Loewen is a sociologist, a graduate of

Harvard, and the author of *Lies My Teacher Told Me: Everything Your American History Textbook Got Wrong*.) According to these authors, Americans' poor knowledge of history can be blamed on the textbooks we used in school and the textbooks children are using now.

James Loewen spent two years at the Smithsonian Institution surveying twelve leading high school textbooks of American history. He found "an embarrassing blend of bland optimism, blind nationalism, and plain misinformation." According to Loewen, textbooks are the dominant tool of the history teacher, and history lessons revolve around the content included in the textbooks. However, according to Loewen, there are several problems with history textbooks:

- **History textbooks are boring.** The very idea that children would willingly want to read a textbook makes most people laugh. Publishers want their textbooks to be adopted by as many states as possible so they dare not write anything that might offend a state. For example, publishers dare not publish anything bad about a president that came from California, or California might not "adopt" (purchase and use in the classroom) their textbooks. And when a publisher writes about the Civil War, they must make both the Northern and the Southern states look good or else those states won't buy their textbooks. This creates textbooks where everyone is a hero and everything has a happy ending. This type of writing makes for pretty bland reading—a history that seems unbelievable and predictable, just like a Hollywood movie.

- **History textbooks don't make kids think.** History is an inexact science; however, history textbooks present events and facts as absolutes. Students are expected to accept the information in textbooks as 100 percent accurate and unbiased without ever questioning the author's intentions or point of view. Students need to learn how to analyze controversial subjects so that they can develop opinions of their own. Parents should encourage their children to become historians themselves, to research the right answers, and not to accept every fact or date without question.

- **History textbooks are used to build character and blind patriotism.** Textbook titles like *Land of Promise, The American Way, Rise of the American Nation,* and *The Great Republic* are designed to make readers proud to be Americans. While there is nothing wrong with bolstering national pride, Loewen and Hakim believe that history textbooks are not necessarily the place to do this. As Loewen humorously points out, chemistry texts are not titled "Rise of the Molecule." When textbooks present America and Americans as infallible and godlike, they do not allow us to learn from our mistakes.

- **History textbooks try to cover everything in one book.** Because textbook publishers are afraid of offending their buyers (the state adoption committees), they dare not leave out any information or detail that might be of concern to a particular group or geographical area. This makes textbooks overly large and overly full of information, and forces history teachers to rush through the material. Teachers have no time to use discussion and debate to assess what students have learned; instead, they assign for homework the fill-in-the-blank questions and "key terms" at the end of each chapter. Consequently, most students remember the information they learned just long enough to answer the questions and pass the test. Students don't retain any real knowledge or feelings about the subject.

- **History textbooks are often inaccurate.** Textbooks say that Ponce de Leon went to Florida to find the fountain of youth, but according to Loewen he went mainly to capture Native Americans as slaves. The story of Columbus, presented by textbooks, is unverifiable. Columbus did not die poor and unaware of what he had accomplished; rather, he died a wealthy man and received the title "Admiral of the Ocean Sea." The voyage to America was not a difficult three-month voyage; it was, according to Columbus's own journal, an easy one-month voyage. Columbus was not the only person to believe that the world was round. According to historical evidence, most of the world at that time knew that the world was not flat. However, these errors are allowed because they make the story more interesting. Homeschoolers have the luxury of time to search out the real story.

- **History textbooks can be racist.** Textbooks have a habit of omitting certain information. For example, textbooks praise Columbus as "brave, wise, and godly." Yet, many Native Americans and African Americans view Columbus differently. Columbus was indeed the first "white" man to discover America. He was also responsible for sending the first slaves across the Atlantic, and according to Loewen, he probably sent more slaves than any other individual. According to the well-known historian Benjamin Keen, "By 1516, thanks to the sinister Indian slave trade and labor policies initiated by Columbus (on Haiti), only some 12,000 (of Haiti's eight million Arawak Indians) remained." By 1542, fewer than 200 Indians were alive and by 1555, they were all gone. Columbus was also responsible for cutting off the hands of any Indian who could not pay a monetary "tribute." These nasty details about Columbus's life are not included in the textbooks. Textbooks also omit information about President Woodrow Wilson's life. Wilson is properly hailed for his legislative accomplishments that included tariff reform, the Federal Reserve Act, the Workmen's Compensation Act, and the League of Nations. However, the textbooks fail to mention that Wilson was an outspoken white supremacist who believed that "blacks" were inferior and ordered that white and black workers in federal government jobs be segregated from one another. Why aren't these details included in the textbooks? No African American would ever consider Woodrow Wilson a hero. Textbooks that present him as such are written from a white perspective. You can turn the various biases of textbooks into a powerful sociological and political lesson.

So what is a parent to do? How can you help your child learn history in a way that is meaningful and memorable? Where in history should you start? With ancient Egypt? With the colonization of America? Should you encourage your child to memorize dates? If textbooks are not a good way to teach history to children, then how can a parent develop their own history curriculum? One that is tailored to their child's interests and age? The following suggestions may help get you started:

- **Study history in a way that makes sense for your child.** Some homeschoolers study history backward, as "What caused this to happen?" Some homeschoolers bounce around in history, studying the topics their child is interested in and eventually tying them all together. Other homeschoolers start with the Old Testament and learn history as "This caused this, which caused this, which caused this." Some homeschoolers study history by subject area. For example, the history of music, the history of sports, etc. The choice is yours. You can explore history in the way that works best for you and your child. Make it exciting.

- **Teach history as a story, not just a collection of facts and dates.** *A History of Us* by Joy Hakim is very popular with homeschoolers because the books are easy to read (written at a fifth-grade level) and use a series of stories to teach American history. Some parents read the books to their children as part of their bedtime reading. These books are graphically appealing with such interesting stories about history that many homeschooling parents have read every single one, and enjoy reading them as much as a good novel. Joy Hakim's books also gave them solid knowledge of the history of the United States, one that their own social studies education did not. They were again excited about history and shared that excitement with their children.

- **Encourage your child to be a history detective.** Read books such as *Lies My Teacher Told Me* and *Mathematical Scandals,* or watch historical movies, and then discuss what you've learned with your children.

- **Separate myths from facts.** According to historians, "Betsy Ross never did anything and she played no role whatsoever in the creation of any actual first flag." Betsy's descendants invented the Betsy Ross myth in 1876 in order to create a tourist attraction in Philadelphia. As an adult, you can learn from sources other than textbooks, such as original documents and autobiographies, and this will make it easier for you to pass on accurate information to your children.

- **Present history from different sources.** No two people are likely to have the same interpretation of any event. Therefore, it's helpful to read historical accounts from people of opposite views, for example, reading about the American Revolution from an American point of view and a British point of view.

- **Help your child create a "century book."** Homeschoolers who follow the Charlotte Mason method oftentimes have their children create a "century book." To make such a book, you simply put paper in a binder and then place the name of the century on the top of the page. When your child learns about certain events or people, she adds a brief description or draws a picture on the appropriate page. In this way, children get a sense as to what happened when.

- **Use the Internet to find "original source" materials.** Thanks to the Internet, your child can read the Declaration of Independence, the Gettysburg Address, and Martin Luther King, Jr.'s "I Have a Dream" speech. Simply type in the name of the event or person you are studying and you will be guided to hundreds of Web sites on that subject. James Loewen suggests that when your child writes a bibliography, he should include one line as to why he believes that source.

- **Use videos, PBS specials, and historical novels to help history come alive.** Just be sure to investigate their accuracy. If you type the name of the video, book, or movie into your Web browser, you are bound to find discussion groups that are debating its authenticity. Once you find the topic you're interested in, you can order it from PBS.org. PBS also has a video catalogue that you can request from their Web site.

- **Make history emotional.** We remember things we have an emotional reaction to. People remember Helen Keller because her story moved them.

History is exciting and horrifying and beautiful and tragic. Show the drama behind the event, not just the dry facts.

- **Make history relevant to the present and to your child's own life.** How has the women's suffrage movement affected your life today? How did the invention of the lightbulb change the way you live today?
- **Introduce fewer topics and examine them more thoroughly.** You do not have to study everything. You do not have to rush. Focus on the big picture and follow your interest until you are ready to move on to another topic.
- **Encourage debate when studying history.** History is not just answers, it is questions too. Which is more accurate, *Roots* or *Gone with the Wind*? Encourage your children to back up their arguments with solid evidence they themselves have researched.
- **Teach your children to question what they read, see, and hear.** Does what they're reading make sense? Why was it written? Whose viewpoint is presented? Is it backed up by original sources? Children today are bombarded with information. They need to learn how to determine what is real and what is not.

You do not have to know everything to teach your child history. Your role is to facilitate their learning and teach them how to teach themselves. For history, that means showing your children how to find books, dissenting opinions, maps, and people who can answer their questions so they can use that information to draw their own conclusions.

HISTORY RESOURCES

- *A History of Us* by Joy Hakim
- *Lies My Teacher Told Me: Everything Your American History Textbook Got Wrong* by James Loewen
- *Thinking Critically About Movies* by Mark Carnes
- *Whatever Happened to Penny Candy* by Richard Marbury

- *The Truth About Columbus*, a poster-book by James Loewen
- The Bluestocking Press catalogue a great source for original source materials and other history products. 1-800-959-8586

YOUNG CHILDREN AND COMPUTERS

Child development experts are in disagreement over whether computers are helpful or harmful to young children. Some of the concerns about computer use include lack of exercise, eye problems, and damage to the young child's developing brain, wrist pain, potential radiation exposure, back pain, and Internet pornography. Repetitive stress injuries—usually sore wrists, tingling fingers, and aching backs—have been found in children as young as eight.

Steve Jobs, the founder of Apple Computer, also has concerns about computer use:* "I used to think that technology could help education, and I've probably spearheaded giving away more computer equipment to schools than anybody else on the planet. But I've had to come to the inevitable conclusion that the problem is not one that technology can hope to solve. Lincoln did not have [Internet access] at the log cabin where his parents homeschooled him and he turned out to be pretty interesting. Historical precedent shows that we can turn out amazing human beings without technology. Precedent also shows that we can turn out uninteresting human beings with technology."

Although most child development and computer experts are comfortable with moderate computer use by older students, they do have the following advice for the parents of young children:

- Do not use your computer as a baby-sitter and sit your child in front of a screen for long periods of time.

---

*This interview with Steve Jobs originally appeared in *The Atlantic Monthly* in an article called "The Computer Decision," by Todd Oppenheimer, July 1997.

- Regardless of the age of your child, use the computer primarily as a research and communications tool—not as a substitute for a human teacher.
- Keep in mind that when children are using the computer, they are not actively using their bodies. Children are meant to move around. Get them outdoors as much as possible.
- Word processing programs, with their spelling and grammar tools, can be helpful for young children who are developing their writing skills. E-mail can also help children connect with others and help them put their ideas and feelings into writing.
- Although the computer can be helpful in some areas, it is no substitute for creative play, reading books, cooking, building things, gardening, and other hands-on experiences of nature and the physical world.
- Be as careful choosing software programs as you are in choosing books. Make sure the program is appropriate for your child's age and development. Make sure your child is learning something.
- Observe your child and see how computer use is affecting her. Trust your observations. If you decide not to let your young child use the computer directly, remember that you can still use it yourself to find answers to her questions, follow up on her interests, take virtual field trips, and develop interesting lesson plans. Our feeling is that you should introduce your children to the computer, just be sure to use it wisely.

CROWD CONTROL FOR LARGE FAMILIES
AND FAMILIES WITH TODDLERS AND INFANTS

Homeschooling families come in all sizes, and it's natural to wonder how parents can guide the education of older children while still giving attention to toddlers and babies. In large families, the older children often help teach their younger siblings, and since teaching is an excellent way to learn something, the older child benefits by developing very strong basic skills. A family with toddlers may opt for either including the child in the activity or distracting them from the activity. Toddlers love to draw at the table and do "real" worksheets while their brothers and sisters are studying, and it's surprising how much they pick up. Some homeschooling parents use educational videos and PBS shows occasionally to occupy their younger children while they are working with someone else.

The longer they practice, the better homeschooling parents get at juggling the homeschooling needs of several children. A parent may listen to one child read aloud while nursing the baby. Or the parent may save one-on-one work with an older child for when younger siblings are napping. Although it can be challenging at first, there are many advantages in homeschooling a large family. Younger children have lots of good role models and learn from the successes and failures of their older siblings. Older children are able to develop close ties with their younger brothers and sisters that they might not have had a chance to develop if they were away at school for long hours each day. Homeschooling does not create perfect children who never compete with or squabble with one another, but it can create close ties between family members who naturally come to know each other better because of the time they spend together.

> "I can't count how many e-mail messages I've received through Homeschool.com from new-to-homeschooling parents who list every book and subject imaginable that they plan to use, then ask me if they've left out anything. 'Whoa, relax,' I tell them. 'Does your child really need to learn about rocket science this year? He's only four years old!'"
>
> **Linda Dobson, *The First Year of Homeschooling Your Child***

The advantage of homeschooling the younger child is that you have time together as a family and he has a chance to enjoy his childhood. It allows you to protect your children a bit longer from the hard realities of school violence, drugs, and consumerism. Children who are homeschooled while they are young grow up with a stronger sense of self, and that confidence will serve them well in their teen years.

SUGGESTIONS FOR HOMESCHOOLING THE YOUNGER CHILD

- Remember, your children will be young for only a short time. Enjoy your time together.
- Delay formal reading instruction until your children are ready, but do read to them every day.
- Let your kids see you using and enjoying math.
- Educate your children to question the history they read and see. Have them ask themselves, "Why is this version of events believable?"
- Make a special effort to involve your children in science projects and classes. Strong science skills are crucial for information age success.
- Let your children set the pace. Design their studies to match their interests.

CHAPTER FIVE

Homeschooling Through High School (Ages Thirteen to Eighteen)

THE NUMBER OF FAMILIES HOMESCHOOLING teenagers has increased over the last few years, and homeschooling for teens is now very common. With today's growing concerns about safety, negative socialization, and low academic standards, more and more parents are turning to home education. Technology has also fueled this growth, as self-instructional software, video curricula, and the Internet have all made homeschooling the older child easier than most parents previously believed.

Some parents discard the idea of homeschooling because they worry that they will not be able to teach their children the tougher subjects like algebra, chemistry, or foreign languages. But remember, you don't have to be your child's only teacher, and as your child grows older you will find your role changing from that of teacher to that of helper or guide.

RECOMMENDED READING

- *Homeschooling the Teen Years* by Cafi Cohen
- *The Teenage Liberation Handbook: How to Quit School and Get a Real Life and Education* by Grace Llewellyn

- *Real Lives: Eleven Teenagers Who Don't Go to School* by Grace Llewellyn
- *Homeschooling the Middle Years* by Shari Henry
- *The High School Handbook* by Mary Schofield
- *Homeschooling the High Schooler* by Diana McAlister and Candice Oneschak

Some parents worry that if their child homeschools through high school, he will miss out on important social events like proms and graduation. As you'll discover in this chapter, however, homeschoolers have beautiful and creative rituals of their own to mark the passages from childhood to adulthood. You also need not worry that your homeschooled child will not be able to get a good job or go to college. Homeschooled teens do exceptionally well on college placement tests and have been accepted into some of the best colleges in the country.

Education and schooling are not necessarily the same thing. History is full of examples of people who have succeeded in life without attending a traditional high school. People as diverse as William Lear, the inventor of the Learjet, and Colonel Harland Sanders, the founder of Kentucky Fried Chicken, all left school early because school wasn't teaching them what they wanted to know. Even more important, not-so-famous students are also doing well and leading happy, fulfilled lives without having completed a traditional high school education.

Homeschooling is a wonderful, liberating option—especially for unhappy teens who are frustrated with the school system. In addition, the teen years can be one of the most exciting times in your child's life, and homeschooling allows you to spend that time with your child to help her discover her place in the world.

"IF I'D ONLY KNOWN _____ WHEN HOMESCHOOLING MY TEEN."

"We started homeschooling when my daughter was a teenager. She was being assaulted in school and was becoming involved in things that were not going to bring her any joy, just lots of pain. I felt she was going to a prison every day. I feared for her life. I began to homeschool my other daughter, who was nine at the time, because there was a new law that said when your child has entered school grounds, she is no longer yours, but is the property of the school. That meant that they could do anything they pleased with her while she was there. I worked as a volunteer right next to the principal's office and saw many things that were not supposed to happen. I quit helping and asked my husband if I could homeschool. When we started it was very difficult. One reason was that my older daughter did not want to homeschool—she even went back to school for a short time. But now I couldn't pay our children to go to a public school."

Leticia—Tucson, Arizona

"Ten years have passed and our oldest is now a married college graduate, our second son is a junior in college, and our youngest is a senior in high school doing dual-credit studies at the community college. The first few years we did all of our work at home with a variety of curriculum. We attended field trips, social activities with the support group, and a 4-H club of homeschool students. Once my oldest hit Algebra 2, I began swapping services with two other homeschool moms. I taught world history, one taught Algebra 2, and the other taught English. During this time we also attended a sports activity day with hundreds of other homeschool families in the Houston area. In 1995, we began the home-directed approach of homeschool by having our boys take some outside classes through a homeschool tutorial program and our boys began taking their math, science, and English classes there. In their junior years of high school, our oldest two boys also took dual-credit classes at the local community college. When they graduated from high school they already had a large amount of college credits. They both went on to college, where they received a variety of scholarships and grants. Some traditional only at-home families might frown on our approach, but I have found these homeschooling classes to be just what we and others have needed when the subject matter becomes too difficult for us to teach. The competitive atmosphere in the small classroom has also helped my competitive-minded boys excel. Our boys have also participated in homeschool sports. Our youngest has hopes of receiving a college scholarship for baseball and has participated in the first two National Homeschool Baseball Tournaments. Our oldest two participated in National Basketball tournaments."

Adel—Kingwood, Texas

"I homeschool three teens, two seniors and one freshman. This is my third year to homeschool. When our girls were in school, the pressure from the other kids was terrible. Not to mention the bomb threats and hit lists and school shootings! Since we have been home-schooling, all that has changed. I know where my kids are, who they are with, and I know what they are doing in school and what they are learning. It is easier for me to know that they are completing their work, I know what they understand, and what they need help with. And we participate in a homeschool group, where we all get together for field trips, play days, Spanish class, etc., so the kids are around other homeschoolers. I personally started a program this year called 'Teen Time.' At least once a month, all the homeschool teens (and their friends) get together for a low cost, fun-filled, get-to-know-each-other time. Last month, we all played volleyball and went swimming. This month, we are meeting on a basketball court to play basketball. I am sold on homeschooling."

Dianne—Heber Springs, Arizona

REASONS TO HOMESCHOOL THROUGH HIGH SCHOOL

- **Efficiency:** Many homeschoolers complete standard high school academics in eighteen to twenty-four months, very quickly compared to the four years most high schools take. Using self-instructional materials they choose, and learning in ways that make sense to them, most teens can cut the time for traditional high school in half.
- **Head Start on College:** Homeschooled teenagers often take college classes to supplement high school homeschooling.
- **Self-Directed Learning:** Most homeschooled teenagers learn not only to teach themselves, they also become expert networkers.
- **Travel:** Freedom from the scheduling constraints of school allows homeschoolers to take advantage of travel opportunities whenever they present themselves.
- **Work Experience:** Teenage homeschoolers have time for volunteer and paying jobs. Often they get better jobs than those who attend school simply because they are available during school hours.
- **Time:** Homeschoolers not only have more hours each day for creative endeavors and learning activities, they also have more time to be alone, to think, to daydream—to develop a private self and a strong personal identity.
- **Family Closeness:** Homeschooling parents almost universally report that their teenagers, in contrast to many adolescents who pull away from their families, grow closer to all family members.
- **Limited Peer Pressure:** Removed from the near-constant peer pressure in schools, most homeschooled teens develop mature manners and values.

- **Fun:** Homeschooling teens is fun for parents, who—in light of their life experience—enjoy learning all the math and history and foreign language they missed the first time around.

—excerpted from *Homeschooling the Teen Years* by Cafi Cohen

TRANSITIONING FROM HOMESCHOOL TO HIGH SCHOOL

It is not uncommon for parents to homeschool their children for elementary school and then send them on to a traditional high school. The advantage of homeschooling your children during their formative years is that you will know for sure they have a solid academic foundation and a strong grounding in your family's values and morals. With this background, they will be better prepared to tackle the challenges and temptations of school life.

If you believe you will eventually enroll your child in a public or private school, plan ahead. Find out what the requirements are for the school they will be attending. According to some homeschooling parents, some high schools have more entrance rules and requirements than college! Find out what your school-of-choice expects and adapt your homeschooling program accordingly.

Set your child up for success by making sure that his academics are on par or advanced for the subjects he will be studying. Make sure your child knows how to create the type of reports schools expect and that he knows how to take tests. If you have done a good job preparing him, he should have no problem with the academics, but will still need some time to make new friends and learn basic classroom rules.

Once your child is taking classes, he may need a few days to a few weeks to adjust to the new atmosphere. If you have done a good job preparing him, he should have no problem with the academics, but will still need some time to make new friends and learn basic classroom rules.

RECOVERING FROM SCHOOL BURNOUT

Just as there is an adjustment period for homeschoolers who begin learning at school, there is also an adjustment period for children who have been learning in a classroom setting for most of their lives and suddenly find themselves learning at home. This transition or adjustment period is commonly referred to as "decompression."

Decompression can last anywhere from a few months to a full year, depending on the number of years the child has spent in school and how negative their experience might have been. For some children, school is an attack on their self-worth, where they, unfortunately, learn not to believe in themselves. This is especially the case for children who were viewed as fat, ugly, poor, stupid, or different in any way. These children need time to recover from their school experiences and to rebuild their confidence. For other children, the experiences may not have been painful, but the child has been trained to do as she is told, work for grades rather than for quality, to learn according to a schedule that may not work well for her, and to learn about subjects for which she has little or no interest. When these students begin homeschooling, the entire family changes the way they view education and life. Suddenly there is time to be alone, time to pursue interests and talents, and time to relax with family and friends. Soon your teen will stop being so competitive and peer-oriented and will become more self-directed and family-oriented. This transition is not always smooth, however, and many homeschooling parents report that when their child comes home from school there is a period where they are tired and uninterested in academics. One homeschooling mom was frustrated because she had spent hours choosing her child's curriculum, only to discover that her son didn't want to do any of it. This is natural, but it can also be frustrating for parents. Some families have dealt successfully with decompression and burnout by giving their child a set amount of time as a "vacation" from chores, lessons, and schoolwork. Once these teens get a taste of freedom, they can begin thinking about what they want out of life and how they want to spend their days. Most homeschooling parents report that they do not have the types of behavioral problems that schools have. If their teen is rebellious, talks back, or refuses to study, they can always go back to school. For most homeschooled teens, doing their studies at home is a privilege, and they know it. Although parents do not use school as a threat, homeschooled teens tend to cherish their new freedom and do not want to give it up.

After this "vacation" period, the parent and child together can determine goals and expectations. This is the time to trust your child and help him learn to trust himself. This is the time to encourage your child and help him develop his curiosity and creativity. Before you know it, your child will once again be hungry for joyful, purposeful learning.

DESIGNING A PERSONALIZED EDUCATION YOUR TEEN CAN GET EXCITED ABOUT

Whether your child is college-bound, business-bound, or undecided, homeschooling allows students to have a high school education that is meaningful, exciting, and as structured or unstructured as you want it to be. Although high-school-level homeschooling tends to be more structured than elementary level homeschooling (even unschoolers tend to organize their homeschool learning), this organization does not have to follow a school-type pattern. Instead, most teenage homeschoolers organize their time to fit their goals. These goals can be big or small, such as finding the perfect geometry textbook by a certain date, reading the newspaper every day, or writing a musical by Easter.

Goal-setting will help your child stay focused on challenging himself instead of doing things from a "have to" mode or out of some fear that he will fall behind if he doesn't do it. Grace Llewellyn, the author of *The Teenage Liberation Handbook*, suggests that students first take a vacation from learning to renew their spirits, then begin doing two hours of academics and four hours of some kind of work or project each day. The rest of the afternoon can be spent reading, visiting friends, talking with parents, cooking, etc. Once the student has tried this type of schedule for a month, he will know how he wants to change it.

Grace Llewellyn also makes the following suggestions on how to develop a learning plan that meets graduation and college entrance requirements:

- *Have your child make a list of the subjects she has to cover.* Have her write down all the ways she can think of to "study" each one, and a list of related books she thinks she might like to read. Encourage her to ask family members and friends for their suggestions.
- *Have him make a list of his most important interests.* Then look at each one and together consider how academic subjects could be related. For instance, if your child loves horses, his list might look like this:
    - *Language Arts/English:* Read *National Velvet.* Write a profile of a local horse breeder. Write poetry or stories from a horse's point of view.
    - *Social Sciences:* Conduct a study of careers related to horses. Look into why so many young girls are intensely interested in horses by conducting a survey or another type of study. Read about the profound influence horses have had on cultures around the world, such as the culture of the Plains Indian tribes. Stay on a working cattle ranch for a week.
    - *Science:* Learn about horse anatomy, diseases, and biology. Find out about the evolutionary history of horses. Learn to use a microscope to diagnose horse diseases.
    - *Art:* Draw horses. Make a saddle or other tack. Produce a documentary video on horse care or horse races. You get the idea.

Let your child's interests drive them along. One homeschooling mother, who wrote about her experiences in *The Teenage Liberation Handbook*, commented:

This past year, we got away from correspondence schools altogether, ordered our own texts (for math only), and really got unschooled. . . . My daughter (thirteen) now studies totally independently, with only occasional help in algebra, or help with Spanish conversation. Her progress is really astounding too. She reads more than ever, and does about three times the work that she did in regular school—by choice. I guess that once we eliminated all the busywork, she discovered how much fun learning could be. She is once again eager, sets her own schedule, and still manages to get so much done that it is truly astonishing. The changes in her have also been very beneficial, because, as she controls and uses her own time, it has matured her and made her very responsible and sensible.

Teach your children to dream big dreams and have big goals. Any lack of skill or experience your child might have can be made up for with time and patience. Adolescents have incredible energy and passion. Show your teen how to direct that energy toward his goals and interests.

RECOMMENDED READING

- *What Color Is Your Parachute?: A Practical Manual for Job-Hunters and Career-Changers* by Richard Bolles
- *Wishcraft* by Barbara Sher
- *The Creative Spirit* by Daniel Goleman
- *Ferguson's Guide to Apprenticeship Programs*, available in the reference section of your library

DEVELOPING SPECIAL INTERESTS

One of the biggest advantages homeschooled teens have over their schooled peers is "time." Homeschooling takes less time than classroom-based learning. Even the most structured homeschooler rarely spends more than two to four hours a day studying. The rest of the time is spent pursuing interests and developing talents. Michelle Bolton is a case in point. She has been homeschooled since the second grade. Because she set her own schedule for schoolwork, practice, and lessons, she was able to enjoy flexibility not available to classroom-bound students. Michelle began playing the French horn when she was thirteen. By the time she was seventeen, she had received an invitation to play at Carnegie Hall in New York City. Her personal talents were allowed to thrive in the homeschooling environment because she had plenty of time to develop her specialty. Even when you add on time for chores, meals, and other daily requirements, homeschooled teens have four to ten hours a day that they can use any way they want.

Some teens use this time to enjoy traditional extracurricular activities like sports, drama club, or music. Others use their time to develop expertise in cooking, ancient history, costume design, chess, horses, sailing, family history, gardening, pottery, and a myriad of other activities. For example, a student who is a budding naturalist may begin by using field guides to help her catalogue the plants, insects, and animals in her own backyard. Sasha Earnheart-Gold, a homeschooler, established a nonprofit group that trains farmers in Bolivia and Mexico to propagate and care for apple trees. His organization received grants and awards that helped fund twelve hundred seedlings being planted and then flown to farmers around the world to feed them and to trade on the world market. Sasha finished high-school-level home education at thirteen, and during one of his work-study-abroad tours he was inspired by someone he met and conceived his company, Apple Tree International. Sasha is currently at Dartmouth and one of his dreams is to travel the globe, sampling apples that his students—farmers in some of the most impoverished regions in the world—have planted.

A teen interested in music might listen to music on her own, participate in a jazz choir at the local community college, take an Internet-based music theory class, and play piano at her church for free and at local restaurants for tips.

For those homeschoolers whose passions include competitive sports, both advantages and disadvantages exist. The student who is serious about an individual sport will probably improve more as a homeschooler than as a school student because he has more time to practice and has the freedom to train with the best coaches in his area, not just the ones at their local high school.

Homeschoolers who want to play on public school sports teams, however, face some hurdles. Some states allow homeschoolers to participate in their sports programs and some do not. If you want your homeschooler to play on a public school team, you will have to plan ahead and find out what the requirements are for your area. The best way to do this is to contact the school and see what its homeschooling policy is. Be advised, however, that spots on these teams can be very competitive and feelings can run very strongly against the homeschooled student. If your child is allowed to participate on a team, he will most likely be required to meet the school's academic requirements. One homeschooler in Wisconsin decided to go to school for the first time in order to be on the school's gymnastics team. After one year, however, she decided to return home because she missed her family and wanted to resume her piano lessons and ballet lessons that she had had to give up because of her school schedule. This family was able to work out a compromise with the Wisconsin Interscholastic Athletic Association, wherein the girl participated not as a homeschooler, but as a transfer student. According to their agreement, the student was required to start taking classes on campus one week before the first meet and to take twenty hours of electives. She did not mind this so much because she was able to take art class, driver's education, and study hall. She remained a transfer student for the length of the gymnastics season, but then returned home after that for full-time homeschooling.

Some homeschoolers choose not to play on public school teams because they do not want their child to have to meet the school's academic requirements. Other homeschoolers choose not to participate because they are afraid that if the state is allowed to regulate a homeschooler's academic requirements because of sports, it is just a matter of time before the state tries to establish all homeschooling requirements.

Some homeschooling families have gotten around the public school sports issue by building up their own homeschooling teams. One family in Pennsylvania started their own basketball league. The first year they had only seven people aged eleven to seventeen. By the team's third year, they had enough players for three teams—one for the seven-to-ten-year-olds, one for the ten-to-thirteen-year-olds, and one for high school–age students. They played small Christian schools and other homeschooling teams in their area.

If you have a child who is gifted in and passionate about sports, plan ahead and be creative. There is no reason that your child cannot receive a first-rate homeschool education and still develop her athletic talents to the fullest.

TACKLING THE TOUGH SUBJECTS

Parents often worry that they will not be able to educate their children at home for high school because they don't feel they can teach the more advanced subjects like trigonometry, physics, and foreign languages. But, as other home-schooling families have discovered, you don't have to be your child's only teacher, and as children grow more mature, they become incredibly adept at teaching themselves. There are also wonderful learning opportunities out in the community, including books, computer programs, college classes, trade schools, Internet courses, and educational videos.

For the Rupp family, in rural Vermont, the tough subjects were not science and math (both parents are scientists); instead, their tough subjects were music, Latin, and Japanese. This family supported their children's interests by finding affordable music teachers and language tutors in their area and by purchasing a self-study language program.

The Ferenga family, in Massachusetts, solved their tough-subject challenges by creating co-op classes in which several homeschool parents and students participate in informal learning get-togethers. For example, Mrs. Ferenga runs a group called "History on Film," where about fourteen kids come over and watch films like *Spartacus* and the controversial movie *Pearl Harbor*. The Ferengas also have a group literature class where the kids read and discuss challenging books like Dante's *Inferno*. Co-op classes are a wonderful way for your child to connect with other homeschooled teens, and these get-togethers can be as challenging as you want them to be.

Just as with young children, teenagers are voracious learners and inexhaustibly curious. They are always asking questions and forcing parents to stretch beyond their own knowledge. That's one of the biggest pleasures in homeschooling—the "let's go look it up" experience—that allows you to learn along with your child. Don't be afraid of the tough subjects. If you're like other homeschooling parents, those will probably end up being your favorites.

VOLUNTEERING, MENTORSHIPS, AND APPRENTICESHIPS

Volunteer work, mentorships, and apprenticeships can be an excellent way for your child to learn more about their areas of interest and to get real-world experiences. With a mentorship, the student learns mostly from an individual. With an apprenticeship, the student learns mostly from the job. Volunteer jobs and mentorships generally do not pay, but apprenticeships can pay. And some formal apprenticeships even confer associate degrees upon successful completion of the training.

Encourage your child to work, not just for money, but for what they can learn from the experience. Are there businesses in your area that your child could visit to learn more about the skills or processes that intrigue him? If your child explains that he is conducting a research project then he may be allowed to follow his mentor around for a while. When approaching a potential mentor, it is helpful to have your child bring along a portfolio of her work in that field. This portfolio can include informal essays on a particular topic, work samples, a list of the books she has read on that topic, letters of reference, and anything else that shows the child's knowledge of the subject and her eagerness to learn more. Have your child think about what she is willing to give in exchange for this learning opportunity. Is she willing to wash test tubes in a lab? Work backstage at the theater? Research and write reports for her local legislator? Potential mentors and apprenticeship providers will be more willing to give your child their time and knowledge if they can see how this can benefit him or her. Homeschoolers have a big advantage here because they are available during school hours, but your child must still convince the company or the mentor that he is there to help, not to steal the mentor's time.

Volunteering, mentorships, and apprenticeships are a great way for your child to see what a job is really like before she spends her time and money on college. These opportunities also help your teen develop a strong work ethic. They can be formal arrangements, tied in with college credit, or they can be casual, informal relationships. You can learn about the child labor laws in your state by contacting the state labor department.

If your child thinks they might want to go to law school, have him find out what it's really like to be an attorney. A child whose passion involves animals may want to volunteer at the Humane Society or help out at a local veterinarian's office. He may start out emptying trash cans, but if he is intelligent and reliable, he may soon be observing and assisting with some of the surgeries.

An eleven-year-old homeschooler was very interested in chemistry, so the mother asked a friend of hers who was a chemist if her son could "hang around" while she worked. The chemist asked her boss. The boss was a college professor who was very interested in homeschooling and gave the eleven-year-old access not only to the chemistry lab but also to the friendly, educated chemist. What a fabulous opportunity to learn science from a real scientist doing real work!

When asking for an internship, apprenticeship, volunteer position, or job, it helps if you suggest a trial period of three weeks or so. Then, if it works out, you can keep going and an employer or mentor is more likely to say yes if the commitment is short-term.

Like so many aspects of homeschooling, you never know where your child's interest may take her. Volunteering, mentorships, and apprenticeships let teenagers discover adult opportunities and real-world experiences before they are out on their own.

JOB AND ENTREPRENEURIAL OPPORTUNITIES FOR TEENS

Some teens move smoothly from school to work. These are the children who always seemed to have known what they wanted to do. Kristine Breck, a homeschooler in Alaska, turned her interest in animals into a rewarding career. Kristine taught herself how to train animals and trained several winning obedience dogs, a performing sheep, the world champion racing reindeer, and her own horse. A traveling "big cat" show came to Alaska, and Kristine introduced herself to the leader and showed him her résumé. After an audition, she and her mother were invited to work with the show permanently in Florida. This happened when Kristine was fourteen years old. When Kristine was fifteen, she traveled with the big cat show without her mother and had full responsibility for herself and her animals. By the time she was nineteen, Kristine had her own performing animal show that traveled throughout the United States, even appearing on *The David Letterman Show.*

Leonie Edwards, at age sixteen, knew she wanted to become a dentist, so she went to work as a dental assistant's assistant. This gave her firsthand experience in her chosen field and gave her two and a half years of dental experience for her college application. She eventually earned college credit for her work and earned money while going to college.* If your son wants to become an electrical engineer he can make a smooth transition into the working world by beginning now. For example, he can become an electrician by age sixteen and a journeyman by age eighteen and work as an electrician while he earns his electrical engineering degree.

Some teens, however, are less certain about what they want to do and what they want to be "when they grow up." They like lots of different things and have never found one thing that they feel they want to stick with for the rest of their lives. Homeschoolers have an advantage in this area because they have time to explore different options. They have time to find (or make) work that they love doing. Don't let children limit themselves by thinking that only certain types of jobs are available to them. Most people, including teenagers, crave the chance to do meaningful work. Teenagers are in a wonderful position because they do not have to support themselves yet. They can invest their time learning skills that will

---

*Kristine Breck and Leonie Edwards's stories originally appeared in *The Teenage Liberation Handbook* by Grace Llewellyn (Lowry House, 1998), pp. 332–333.

later provide interesting work, or gradually building up a business, or getting started in a field through volunteering. While they are teenagers, they can afford the time to explore their interests and find or create the work they love.

Starting a business can also be the right path for some teens. For the most part, any business that an adult can run, a teenager can run. Since most new businesses do not make a profit the first year, teenagers again have an advantage because they are living with their parents and can afford to learn from their mistakes. Some of the businesses popular with homeschoolers include music lessons, tutoring, and computer work. Computer work is particularly popular with teens because the work pays well and the clients don't care about your age, only about what you know. One homeschooler even created a multimillion-dollar computer business. At age twenty-three, Aaron Fessler created a computer company called Allegro, which he later sold for $55 million.

Many people spend their entire lives feeling trapped, doing work they hate. Perhaps people develop this mentality in school, where they are trapped for twelve years, whether they like it or not. Homeschooled teens have the freedom to approach life and learning in a different way. They can feel passionately about their studies and about their life. One of the most important gifts you can give your teenager is the belief that he can do work that is fulfilling and satisfying, and still put food on the table. Begin now, by showing your child the endless possibilities around him. Use your research skills to find people who enjoy what they are doing. In the same way that you have learned to think "outside the box" concerning your child's education, you can learn to think outside the box concerning their future career. You can help them develop their interests and talents so that they can spend their lives doing what they love.

THE ABCS OF COMPLETION:
GED, PROFICIENCY EXAMS, AND DIPLOMAS

Children who attend traditional schools have very clear milestones that mark the completion of high school and the beginning of college or work. For homeschoolers, who often work and take college classes while still in high school, the division between childhood and adulthood is less distinct, and sometimes families are unsure just how to define graduation.

Some homeschoolers use a traditional "unit-based" method for determining graduation. When the student has completed a certain number of units for each course, the child can "graduate." Students who use independent-study programs graduate when they have met the requirements of that school. Alternatively, some parents adopt the graduation requirements of private schools, like parochial schools, Waldorf schools, or the international baccalaureate program. Some families use testing, like the GED or high school proficiency exams, to determine successful completion, and some decide that their child has graduated from high school when he or she is admitted to college. Other families prefer a more natural transition, where the child gradually continues her studies into college. As a home educator, you are not locked into someone else's goals and someone else's idea of success—you can choose the type of completion that is most meaningful for you and your family.

Even though homeschooled teens spend only two to four hours a day on formal studies, they are often able to complete their graduation requirements in two years instead of four. This means that many homeschooled teens graduate from high school between the ages of fifteen and seventeen. This gives the student plenty of time to explore the world of work, create their own business, or prepare for college.

Some students prepare for college by participating in "dual enrollment" programs. Dual enrollment programs allow a student who is a junior or senior in high school to take classes at a community college and earn both a diploma and a two-year associate degree from the college—at the same time. In some cases, tuition is paid for by the state, since the student is considered to be a public school student, not a homeschooler. Call the admissions office of your local community college to see if dual enrollment is a possibility in your state.

When employers and college officials ask for a diploma, they do not specify that the diploma has to come from an accredited school. Most homeschools are considered to be private schools, so if a child needs a diploma, the parents—as administrators of that school—can create their own certificate. A family in Florida patterned their diploma after the local public school. It acknowledged that the student had completed his requirements and was signed by the important people in their lives, the pastor of their church and their church's homeschool coordinator. It was created more for the student than for schools or employers. If your family grants its own diploma, your child can answer yes to the diploma question on job applications.

Colleges rely mostly on transcripts, test scores, and letters of recommendation. Most college applications don't ask about a diploma because for the most part, the applicant is still in high school and doesn't have one yet. Employers care mostly about experience, but if the job application asks your child if they have a diploma, they can honestly answer yes. Seldom does anyone ask to see the actual document, and most do not care whether the school was accredited or not. Military recruiters care more about diplomas than anyone else. If you know that your child wants a career in the army, navy, marines, or air force, you may want to enroll him in an accredited independent study program or make sure they earn a certain number of college credits while in high school. Your local recruiter can give you specific details.

Graduation is often more meaningful for homeschoolers because it is very personal. The Shelton family created a graduation ceremony for their son Tory that was meaningful and unique. Barb Shelton writes:

Purple, gray, and black balloons and streamers bedecked the room and helped welcome the graduate as he walked up the aisle to "Pomp and Circumstance" wearing a black cap and gown, with a tassel of purple, gray, and black—the "homeschool colors" we chose fifteen years ago! Tory sat in a chair on one side of the "stage," facing the audience and whoever was at the microphone. Dave (Dad) opened the ceremony with comments about our years of homeschooling with the grad, followed by my own comments of a similar nature.

We then had a candle ceremony called "Grandparents' Legacy," where Dave and I shared what each of our parents had given us that we want to pass along to our son. . . . As I gave my dad a green candle, I told him it reminded me not only of his love of the woods, but also of his lifelong love of learning and his continual growth. . . . I asked a few people to share just a bit about Tory—anything they wanted to commend him on, encourage him for his future, "personally impart" to him, what they saw in him that they wanted to bless, etc. . . . (Tory's sister sang two songs).

After this, Tory responded from his heart, and then presented Mom with roses and Dad with a gift. A friend commented to me: "It was so wonderful and encouraging to see Tory thank his parents for home-schooling him and for raising him the way they did. The tears he displayed throughout the graduation also added to the specialness of it all."

Your child's graduation can be anything she wants it to be. It can be a private ceremony, like the one described above, or it can be a group graduation like those sponsored by local support groups. If your child is not interested in any ceremony, he can choose a trip or some other activity that serves as a rite of passage.

IF YOU HAVE AN UNHAPPY TEEN

For some teens, school is an unhappy place where they feel helplessly trapped and miserable. These unhappy teens do not do well in school and sometimes think of themselves as stupid. They may use cigarettes, alcohol, drugs, or hang out with bad crowds as a way to escape their prison. Other teens are not miserable in school, just bored. These students are ready to be out in the world, but still have one, two, or three years of school left. These are the teens who believe in education and get decent grades but can't tell you anything they learned in the past year. For these students, choir, art class, and sports are the only things that make school worthwhile and bearable.

If you have an unhappy teen or a teen who is bored with school, know that it doesn't have to be that way. Homeschooling is a viable option. The teens you've been reading about in this chapter are not gifted; they are just ordinary kids. The difference is that these kids have had the time and freedom to discover their passions and develop their talents.

If you have an unhappy teen, you probably worry about him. You worry that if he doesn't finish high school, he'll be a failure. And you want him to finish what he starts and you think that a diploma will help build up his self-confidence. These are legitimate concerns and aspirations. But maybe school isn't the right choice for your teen. Maybe he would learn better on his own or with you as his guide.

In general, our society has low expectations for teenagers. We have strict curfews to keep them off the streets at night and require them to carry special passes or permits if they are out of school during school hours. In the old days, teens were valued, often joining their parents at work. Today we confine them to institutions with Cyclone fences, barbed wire, and metal detectors.

If your child wants to leave school, perhaps you should consider it. We receive lots of letters from teens who want to homeschool but are afraid their parents won't understand. Try to be open-minded. Ask your child *why* she wants to homeschool and ask her to tell you how she plans to structure her day. Ask her also to respect your concerns. Together, you can come up with a plan that makes sense for both of you.

There are lots of good reasons to homeschool your child, but for the high school student, "freedom" and "time" outshine and surpass all the other reasons combined. Instead of "dropping out" of school, your child can "drop in" to homeschooling and enjoy more control over his life. According to one homeschooler: "Comparing me to those who are conventionally schooled is like comparing the freedoms of a wild stallion to those of cattle in a feed lot."* You *can* homeschool your child through high school. And your child may benefit in ways you never anticipated. If he has successfully homeschooled through high school, life can present many exciting options for him—college or another higher-learning experience could be the next step on his unique journey to adulthood.

---

*This quote originally appeared in *The Teenage Liberation Handbook*, p. 39.

THINGS TO KEEP IN MIND WHEN HOMESCHOOLING A TEEN

- Homeschooling is faster than classroom learning and your teen will only need two to four hours a day for formal studies.
- Encourage your teen to get real world experience via apprenticeships, internships, and volunteer work.
- Encourage your teen to learn history, not from textbooks, but from letters, autobiographies, and other original sources.
- Support your teen's passions and help him become an expert in his areas of interest.
- Strong math, science, and computer skills will help your teen succeed in the information age.
- Your teen may not need a college degree in order to succeed in life. (Read more about this in the next chapter.)

CHAPTER SIX

College and Uncollege Alternatives

Homeschoolers have been admitted to hundreds of colleges throughout the country, including Ivy League schools like Harvard and Yale, large and small state universities, technical institutes such as California Polytechnic, small religious colleges, and military academies. So rest assured that your homeschooler can get into a good college if that is what she chooses to do. Being homeschooled will not diminish her chances for a slot in some of the top universities, and as a matter of fact, it often enhances them.

Homeschoolers' success in college admissions stems from what one Stanford admissions officer calls "academic vitality."

COLLEGE SUCCESS FACTS

- Homeschoolers scored highest on the ACT, higher than public school and private school students.
- Homeschoolers scored highest on the SAT college exams, higher than public and private school students.

- MIT admitted 7 of 21 homeschoolers who applied in the year 2000, an acceptance rate of 33 percent, which is twice the overall acceptance rate.
- The average homeschooler's SAT score is 1100, 80 points higher than the average score. Several homeschoolers have received perfect scores.

According to the Stanford admissions Web site: "We look for a clear sense of intellectual growth and a quest for knowledge in our applicants. What is their level of intellectual vitality? Homeschooled students may have a potential advantage in this aspect of the application since they have consciously chosen and pursued an independent course of study." When asked to offer comments on Linda Dobson's book *Homeschoolers' Success Stories,* Jon Reider, Stanford's former senior associate director of admissions, noted how the profiled homeschoolers in this book had led "an examined life" and further stated that "in the face of enormous cultural pressure, they learned to find their own ways, through trial and error more than through ideology." Homeschoolers are also welcomed into the halls of higher learning because they are eager to learn and are self-directed. They do not hesitate to ask questions and are good at finding answers. Homeschoolers know what they want and expect college to help them achieve their goals. They are also used to controlling their own schedules and establishing priorities. In short, homeschoolers make good college students.

"IF I'D ONLY KNOWN _____
WHEN PREPARING FOR COLLEGE."

"There is no doubt in my mind that children can receive a better education through homeschooling. Currently, I am enrolled as a senior at the University of California-Davis, majoring in microbiology.

For me, homeschooling prepared me for college by teaching me self-motivation, time management, and academics. I also learned a lot by helping out in our family business (a café). This taught me principles of money management and of business. I also was able to interact with the adults who were associated with the business. This is an experience that would not have been available to me if I had gone to public school, and I believe the experience had a positive influence on me. A thirteen-year-old homeschooling friend of mine is also getting this type of experience by volunteering in the entomology department at UC Davis. I don't think he would be able to do this if he was not homeschooled."

Brent—Elk Grove, California

GETTING READY FOR COLLEGE

Even though students make the college decision when they are eighteen or nineteen years old, the preparation for college begins when the student is still in high school. Many homeschoolers begin preparing for college and taking community college classes in the ninth grade. These classes show the student's readiness for college and their ability to perform college-level work, and since homeschooled teens are used to learning independently, they tend to be emotionally ready for college at a younger age. The midteens are also a good time to begin looking into the college application and scholarship process. If your child has a pretty good idea which college he would like to attend and/or which subjects he would like to emphasize, he can adapt his high school studies to meet that college's requirements.

Although colleges and universities welcome homeschoolers, they expect the homeschooled applicant to prove that she is just as well educated as the traditionally schooled applicant and that she can perform well in college. Homeschooling families have reported success with both transcripts and portfolios.

Transcripts list courses and often credits and grades. Portfolios, on the other hand, resemble scrapbooks and may include work samples, awards, photos, reading lists, outside classes taken, and certificates earned. If your child is enrolled in an independent study program, the program provides transcripts and the diploma. Most homeschoolers prepare their own materials.

If you decide to create your own transcript know that all transcripts look different and if your transcript is well made, it will not stick out. Cafi Cohen's book *And What About College?* has detailed directions for how to create your own transcript.

Some colleges prefer to see portfolios, so be sure to contact the college of your choice to see which method they prefer. You may end up submitting transcripts to some colleges and portfolios to others. If your child has attended a junior college, you may use a record of these classes as your transcript. Letters of recommendation are very important, so make sure that your child's recommendations detail your child's accomplishments without sounding overly "gushing."

If your teen is considering college, you will also want to become familiar with the various college admissions tests that are used by colleges throughout the country. The PSAT is taken in the fall of the junior year (or age sixteen) and is used to qualify students for National Merit Scholarships. The SAT-I is the newest version of the SAT and contains tests of mathematical and verbal reasoning. The SAT-II (which used to be called the achievement test) tests for specific subject knowledge in writing, biology, American history, and other subjects and is used mainly by Ivy League colleges like Harvard and Stanford. The ACT is used mainly by colleges in the Midwest and South. A few homeschoolers also take Advanced Placement (AP) and College Level Examination Program (CLEP) tests, which convert good scores into college credit. Test preparation books, like those published by Kaplan or Princeton Review, are available in bookstores and can help homeschoolers (who might not be used to taking tests) learn how to think like the test makers. One last word of advice: Give your teen plenty of time to prepare for these tests. Your child may not be used to taking tests and may need extra time for practice tests.

Historically, homeschoolers do very well on college admissions tests and outperform publicly and privately educated students. According to ACT achievement test reports, while the average composite score of American high school students taking the ACT test was 21, homeschooled teens scored 22.8 (out of a possible 36). Research shows that high achievement on the ACT strongly indicates a "greater likelihood of success in college." Success on the ACT test also reveals that the courses taken by high school students to prepare for college have been effective. Homeschoolers also placed higher than private school students and public school students on the SAT college entrance exams in the year 2000.

In addition to academic success, homeschoolers have also met with athletic success in college. Coaches are recruiting homeschooled athletes and in 2001 the National Collegiate Athletic Association (NCAA) declared about one hundred homeschooled students eligible for athletics as freshmen at major universities, up from eighty-five the year before.

If your child will be applying for financial aid or scholarship money, be advised that homeschoolers apply for these in the same way as everyone else. There is no disadvantage or advantage to being a homeschooler except that your child may have had the time to develop superior skills in some areas that might qualify them for special awards or scholarships.

A "co-op education" can also help you keep costs down. This option is becoming increasingly popular because it combines work and schooling. The student participating in a co-op program will spend two thirds of their school days in a classroom and one third of their time working off their tuition at a local company. Some programs have the students alternating their schedules: one semester in the classroom, the next semester at work. In other programs, the student schedules his work around his school schedule. The typical student of a co-op program graduates in four years, with two to three years of work experience to put on his résumé. Other statistics are equally impressive. According to the National Commission for Co-op Education, 80 percent of co-op students have an easy time getting their first job and they finish school with less debt. Unlike internships, co-ops pay (usually about $7,000 a year) and most programs also give college credit for work hours. To learn more about co-op programs, contact the admissions office of the college of your choice. About 85 percent of the top one hundred Fortune 500 companies offer co-op programs, so there is a lot to choose from.

As homeschooling parents you may have an advantage when it comes to sleuthing out scholarships, grants, loans, and other money-saving options because you are used to researching and finding what you need for your child's education. Money is available in unusual places, so begin early and use your research skills to find the financial support you need.

If your child is not interested in college, or if you can't afford to send your child to college, keep reading, there are alternatives available. These alternatives are particularly well suited to homeschoolers who are used to "thinking out of the box" and make it possible for your child to create a profitable, creative, and meaningful future—without a college degree.

UNCOLLEGE ALTERNATIVES

A growing number of homeschoolers are beginning to ask the obvious question: If homeschooling works so well for elementary school and high school, can't it work well for college too? Can't I continue to give myself a first-rate education without going to college?

RECOMMENDED READING

- *And What About College?* by Cafi Cohen
- *Bear's Guide to Earning College Degrees Nontraditionally* by John Bear
- *The Question Is College: On Finding and Doing What You Love* by Herbert Kohl
- *The Uncollege Alternative* by Danielle Wood
- *Self University* by Charles D. Hayes
- *Cool Colleges for the Hyper-Intelligent, Self-Directed, Late Blooming, and Just Plain Different* by Donald Asher

In America today students are being told that they must go to college to succeed. However, according to Danielle Wood, the author of *The Uncollege Alternative,* there are more college graduates than there are jobs that require a college degree, and 20 percent of college graduates are "underemployed," working in jobs that do not require a degree. College isn't the door opener it once was.

There are good reasons and bad reasons to go to college. If your child loves being in a classroom or wants to become a doctor, college is the right choice for them. There are also bad reasons to go to college, and every year thousands of kids go off to college because they don't know what else to do. Which is understandable. It is the rare person who knows what they want to do with the rest of their life when they are only eighteen years old. And given the cost of a college education and the sacrifices you as parents are going to make to pay for that education, it makes sense to think about whether or not your child really needs a college degree.

According to Danielle Wood:

> College may give you four years to park yourself, but the meter's running, make no mistake. . . . Students who get out of school in four years take with them an average debt of $13,200. That's a pretty heavy load, considering that the average starting salary for graduates with a bachelor's degree is only $22,000. . . . According to a study by the National Center for Education Statistics, more than 30 percent of students who enter college don't return for their sophomore year. Three out of four students who enter college haven't snagged a degree five years later. These are scary numbers. Especially when you consider the debt involved.

There are faster, easier, and less expensive ways to learn that do not require you to be on a college campus. As discussed in Chapter Five, internships and apprenticeships are a great way to get a taste of the adult world. Travel is also a wonderful option, and it doesn't have to be expensive. If your child is unsure at all about going to college, or if you want to explore all the options before you start paying college tuition, consider the following uncollege alternatives:

Time Off

Your child may benefit by taking time off before she starts college. This will give her a chance to think about what she wants to do with her life and may prevent her from entering college just because she doesn't know what else to do. College is not a competition to see who finishes first. There is no harm in taking a break from formal studies until ready to hit the books in earnest. This will give your child a chance to see that there are lots of ways of expanding the mind that have nothing to do with school. Your child may never have the kind of freedom she has now. Before she knows it, she will have a spouse, children, and other responsibilities and obligations that make it difficult to take time off for personal pursuits. It's okay if your child doesn't know what she wants to do. It's when you don't know what you want, during those periods of not knowing, that you are most open to the possibilities. Life is a process, not a destination. Tell your child that it's okay to say "I'm not sure what I'm going to do next. I'm exploring lots of options." Show your child the importance of choosing the kind of life she wants, not just the kind of job she wants. Ask her to consider not just what she wants to do, but who she wants to be, where she wants to live, and why she wants these things.

Travel

If your child is willing to work as he goes, he can see the world—without breaking into his college fund. The first thing he needs to decide is where he wants to go. No matter where, there probably is someone there willing to hire them. And encourage your child to add a little adventure to his travels. The Center for Interim Programs sends people to exotic places to do meaningful work, like working in an orphanage in Jordan, teaching English on a faraway island, or helping out at a wildlife sanctuary. Churches also have opportunities for young adults who want to help out with overseas missions. Or perhaps your child is just looking for fun and would like to work for Club Med or on a cruise ship. If your child has saved the money and is looking for a break, a round-the-world airplane ticket is just $1,000–$2,000, with unlimited stops as long as you keep going in the same direction. Whether traveling for fun or working his way around the globe, your child's world will expand and he may figure out who he really is.

TRAVEL RESOURCES

- *Six Months Off* by Hope Dlugozima
- *The Backdoor Guide to Short-Term Job Adventures* by Michael Landes
- *Time Out* by Robert Gilpin
- *Make a Mil-Yen: Teaching English in Japan* by Don Best, available at 1-800-947-7271
- Club Med Job Hotline
  1-407-337-6660
  www.clubmed.com
- Alliances Abroad
  (an international job placement agency)
  1-888-6-ABROAD
  www.alliancesabroad.com
- The Center for Interim Programs
  1-617-547-0980
  www.interimprograms.com
- Council on International Educational Exchange
  1-800-448-9944
  www.ciee.org

Student Exchange Programs

Your child can become an exchange student for a year or more. The Council on International Educational Exchange can help your child find a friendly family to live with. Or, you can trade students with an overseas homeschool family by placing an ad in a homeschooling magazine or on Homeschool.com's student exchange bulletin board. Homeschooling is becoming increasingly popular in countries like Australia, Japan, South Africa, England, and Canada, and many of these families would welcome the chance to establish a student exchange with homeschoolers in other countries. There are benefits to this type of exchange for both the student and the hosting family. Young people who live overseas pick up the language incredibly fast and they get a chance to immerse themselves into a culture completely, accompanied by the safety and comfort of a kind family. Families who host foreign exchange students also benefit by introducing their children to a new culture and a new language from their own home.

Internships

Internships can take your child from inexperienced to experienced so quickly that your child may not even need college. Internships are also a great way for your child to test the likability of a possible career and can even help them get hired. According to a recent survey from the College Placement Council, three out of ten new hires were former interns, some of who were not college graduates. With internships, you are paying to learn, not with money, but with time. So encourage your child to make the most of it. If she wants to be hired by the company she interns for, she has to make herself irreplaceable. If your child is not hired by the company she interns for, she will still have gained valuable knowledge and experience.

INTERNSHIP RESOURCES

- Environmental Careers Organization has a list of over 650 paid environmental internships.
  www.eco.org
- *America's Top Internships* by Mark Oldman

- *The Internship Bible* by Mark Oldman
- www.internshipprograms.com
- www.rsinternships.com
- www.jobtrack.com

Apprenticeships

Apprenticeships can give your child hands-on experience and a valuable skill. Many chefs, carpenters, electricians, and actors got their start by apprenticing themselves to a "master." Instead of going to school and reading about how to do something, apprentices actually do it. The U.S. Department of Labor regulates apprenticeships, and a list of "official" apprenticeships is available from the Bureau of Apprenticeships and Training at 1-415-975-4007. Your child can also arrange her own apprenticeship if she knows what she wants to learn, whom she wants to learn with, and what she is willing to do in exchange for the training.

Trade School

For some students, trade schools are the ticket to the job they want. Vocational education has a bad reputation, but there are some excellent vocational programs out there that can give your child a cutting-edge education in a fraction of the time and for a fraction of the cost it would take in college. According to the National Center for Educational Statistics, there are over seven thousand vocational schools in the United States, providing educations in health care, business and management, engineering technologies, protective services, and visual and performing arts. A trade school may be the best choice for your child if she wants to become a cosmetologist, dental technician, massage therapist, computer programmer, midwife, or a myriad of other jobs that require specific expertise.

VOLUNTEER RESOURCES

- Americorps
  1-800-942-2677
  www.americorps.org
- Camphill Villages
  (villages for the developmentally disabled in 90 locations across
  the world)
  www.camphillassociation.org
- American Red Cross
  www.redcross.org
- VISTA
  1-202-606-5000
  www.americorps.org/vista
- National Civilian Community Corps
  1-202-606-5000
  www.americorps.org/nccc

Volunteering

Children can help the world and help themselves at the same time. There are lots of programs run by both public and private organizations that help young people broaden their world and discover that there's more to life than just earning and spending money. Americorps, including their VISTA and National Civilian Community Corps divisions, connect volunteers with various nonprofit operations and can be reached at 1-800-942-2677. Their brochure has listings of nonprofits in need of volunteers. The average Americorps program pays volunteers a stipend of $8,000–$15,000 a year, plus a $5,000 educational award. Teach for America pays the most money, between $20,000 and $30,000, plus the educational award. Volunteering may not pay much money, but it can help your child test out the world and find their place in it. Instead of paying a lot of money for a college education, they will be earning a little money doing good and getting the education of a lifetime.

The Military

Believe it or not, the military can train your child to become a photographer, a journalist, or a translator—not just a soldier, sailor, or pilot. The military offers training and work experience for almost two thousand occupations, in exchange for a four- to six-year enlistment commitment. They also pay about $20,000 in college or vocational school tuition. To participate in these programs, your child will have to take the Armed Services Vocational Battery, which is like a career version of the SAT.

Self-Employment

A college education may not be necessary if your child has the vision and the drive to start his own business. A bit of start-up cash is helpful too. The Small Business Administration is the nation's single largest financial backer of small businesses. It can help your young entrepreneur write up a business plan and explore various business ideas with seasoned professionals. There are also a number of organizations that help with funding, like the Capital Environmental Network (which helps environmentally friendly start-ups get funding), Technology Capital Network (which helps high-tech start-ups), and Investor's Circle (44 percent of the entrepreneurs who present at their meetings get funding). A franchise may also make it possible for your child to own his own business without having to start from scratch and without having to learn from his mistakes. You probably know if your child is an entrepreneur if he's been starting his own businesses since he was in grammar school—everything from lemonade stands and lawn mowing to baby-sitting services. If your child's business fails (and a lot of small businesses do fail), he can start again, before he has marriage, parenting, or other responsibilities. And if he discovers he doesn't like owning his own business, and decides to go to college, he'll make better use of his time there.

ENTREPRENEUR RESOURCES

- Small Business Administration
  1-800-827-5722
  www.sbaa.net
- The International Franchise Association
  1-202-628-8000
  www.franchise.org
- Environmental Capital Network
  1-734-996-8387
  www.bizserve.com/ecn
- Investor's Circle
  1-415-929-4900
  www.icircle.org
- Technology Capital Network
  1-617-253-2337
  www.tcnmit.org

HOW TO GET A FREE COLLEGE EDUCATION

If you have drive and determination, you can homeschool yourself through college without having to pay a dime in tuition.

Cindy read everything in the library on geology, including very advanced subjects, for three years. And she enjoyed every minute of that reading. Now she volunteers one day a month at local elementary schools, presenting special science programs she has created. She hopes her contribution will encourage more kids to study science. And she is no longer working at an office job but is a lab technician at a geological engineering firm. She is also an active member of the local astronomy society and has had one article published in that field. All without a college degree.*

Cindy always wanted to be an astronaut but she was past NASA's age limit, thirty-six. So she thought about why she wanted to be an astronaut and discovered that it was because she wanted to go to another planet and study what the planet was made of. So she decided to study geology and eventually to specialize in planetary geology. You might think a person must have a college degree to teach, but Cindy was able to get a job teaching geology without a college degree or credentials. Her employer was so impressed by her experience, he waived the paperwork. And she didn't spend a dime on college classes or get into debt with student loans.

B. R. Christensen was inspired to write *Getting a Free Education Without the High Cost of College* because a friend of hers had been successful getting a high-ranking executive position without having to get an M.B.A. Here's how her friend did it. First of all, this man knew exactly what he wanted to do. He wanted to become director of marketing for a leading software company. He began his education by contacting Harvard University and finding out which courses he would have to take and which books he would have to read in order to earn their M.B.A. degree. He also contacted people who were currently working in marketing and software development and asked them for recommendations of seminars they thought he should attend and books they thought he should read. He put together a notebook that chronicled everything he did and everything he read. When he felt he was sufficiently knowledgeable, he approached a software company and volunteered to work for them free for six months. They were impressed with his determination and resolve and granted his request. At the end of the internship, he began his job hunt. According to this man "companies fell over themselves to hire him" and over time he became director of marketing for an educational software company. All this without a formal college education. This ex-

*Cindy's story originally appeared in *Getting a Free Education Without the High Cost of College* by B.R. Christensen (Effective Living Publishing, 1994).

perience is also welcome news to those who may not be able to afford college. With planning and self-determination, your child can give herself the equivalent of a Harvard education—for free.

One of the assumptions in our society is that you have to have a college degree in order to get a good job. Although you may have to go to medical school to become a doctor, other professions do not require a formal college degree. For example, in some states, people who have experience in the legal field can take the bar exam and become an attorney without having to go to law school.

Experience and knowledge are quickly becoming more important than a person's college degree, which makes sense when you consider the rapid changes taking place in our society today. Six years ago no one had heard of the Internet and there was no such thing as a Web master. In some fields, like business and technology, the information students learn in college is obsolete by the time they graduate.

Self-education is the best type of education. Because in teaching yourself, you get to follow your interests and learn in the way that works best for you. Best of all, you will gain self-confidence and will know that from now on you can learn about anything you want.

Even if your child graduates from college, he will probably need to reeducate himself several times during his lifetime, and his homeschooling experiences are going to help him. He will not need to return to college every time he wants to change jobs or careers. He will be able to reeducate himself and continue to learn all throughout his life.

COLLEGE AND UNCOLLEGE TIPS

- Before your teen decides on a definite career path, have her spend some time watching and interviewing people who work in that field. This way, she'll know what the job is really like and it may prevent her from spending time and money on a job that may not be a good fit for her.

- Your child may not need college in order to achieve his dreams. If you can't afford college, or if your teen does not enjoy classroom learning, see if he can get the experience and knowledge he needs through an internship, an apprenticeship, or through volunteer work.
- Give yourself at least a year to prepare for college. The entire process will be more enjoyable, less stressful, and more fun if you have time for practice tests and financial aid research.
- There are scholarships out there for everything! A reference librarian can help you find books that list college scholarships, grants, and other awards. You may send out a hundred applications, but the financial rewards will be worth it.

CHAPTER SEVEN

Finding Your Child's Special Genius

"IN THE EARLY 1950S, IN A KITCHEN, *a mother stands opening cans and emptying the contents into a pressure cooker. Her son, a Boy Scout, wants to get a merit badge in filmmaking. His father had bought him a super-8 movie camera. Then the child got the inspiration to make a horror movie. For one shot he needs red, bloody-looking goop to ooze from kitchen cabinets. So his mother buys thirty cans of cherries and dumps the cherries into the pressure cooker, rendering a delightfully oozy red goop.*

His mother is not the type who says "Go outside and play. I don't want that stuff in the house." She is more than obliging and she gives him free rein of the house, letting him convert it into his film studio—moving furniture around, putting backdrops over things. She helps him make costumes and even acts in his films. When he wants a desert scene, she drives him out to the desert in their Jeep.

The goopy bloody kitchen scene, she recalled much later, left her picking cherries out of the cupboards for years. Her son's name? Steven Spielberg."

What if Steven's mother never let him mess up the house? What if she hadn't let him use her things as props or didn't take him to locations for shooting his

---

*Steven Spielberg's story is from *The Creative Spirit* by D. Goleman, P. Kaufman, and M. Ray (Penguin Group, 1992).

movies? Would Steven Spielberg have become one of the world's most famous filmmakers? While you hopefully don't have to put cherries into a pressure cooker, what hidden talents and passions does your child have that are just waiting for your support and encouragement? Find out.

Throughout this book, we have advised that as you educate your child at home, you should always consider your child's learning style, interests, multiple intelligences, talents, and passions—the things that make her a unique human being. But forget, for a moment, about all this talk of your child's future success. Instead, just think back to the first moment your eyes slowly took a visual inventory of your infant from head to toe. You knew your child was special. If you can provide an education at home that acknowledges her uniqueness, doesn't your child deserve it?

DISCOVERING YOUR CHILD'S LEARNING STYLE

Learning styles are often categorized or listed as the same as intelligences. They are not the same. Here is the difference: a learning style is how your child takes in information. This is an inborn process and does not change for the rest of a child's life. Intelligence is what your child knows, and this intelligence changes and expands throughout life. A learning style is a child's natural point of entry into the learning process. You can enhance learning by understanding how your child learns, and you can help him develop his competencies by stimulating the myriad of his intelligence potentials.

If a child learns best by listening, it can be assumed that from math to music, she will use her ears to help her understand more about her world. Discover your child's inborn learning style. Let her know what it is. Help her select products and materials that work best for that learning style. This knowledge will lay the foundation for her to become a lifelong learner. Learning will be natural and exciting to her. The basic three learning styles are auditory, visual, and kinesthetic.

Auditory learners process information by listening and talking. They enjoy listening to audiotapes, verbal instructions, lectures, and music. If your child loves listening to Grandma's stories and often can't wait until the end of a story before they want to ask questions, they most likely are an auditory learner.

Kinesthetic learners learn by touch and movement. They like to touch everything they are interested in. If your child likes to build things, they could very well be a kinesthetic learner. Also called a hands-on learner, these children need plenty of opportunities to build, touch, and explore "real life" equivalents of what they are learning about.

Visual learners learn by seeing and observation. They "see" what they are learning about in their head and often think in pictures. Ask a visual learner to describe a new project they are involved in and they will most likely draw a picture of it. Visual learners have a vivid imagination and can visualize something often before they can describe it. Visual learners get great inspiration from reading, writing, art, and graphs.*

Use these three basic modalities of learning styles as a guide. Observe your child and try to determine their learning style. It is often visible in "what they naturally like doing" or what they are drawn to. For example, if your daughter enjoys listening to Grandma tell stories about growing up in the "good old days," enjoys listening to audiotapes, and likes to verbalize information that was presented to her, then she most likely is an auditory learner. She processes information and communicates information by listening. If your son loves to build models, work with clay, spends hours making space cities using LEGOs, and likes to explore everything interesting by touch, he processes information by touching. He is most likely a kinesthetic learner. Does your child become impatient when extensive listening is required? Or spend hours drawing beautiful pictures that tell a story? Does he stare, doodle, and always find something to watch? Then he is a visual learner and "thinks in pictures."

Keep in mind that learning styles (and the intelligences described on pages 137–8), are not an exact science, and many theories exist in these areas. Observe

*For a complete characteristic checklist, see *Teaching Through Modality Strengths: Concepts and Practices* by Walter Barbe (Zaner Bloser, 1979).

your child and see if you can discover her natural learning style by determining her first movement or process of learning about something that interests her. Is it by movement, seeing, or listening? Use this knowledge when you would like to help her learn new material or acquire a skill. Find the right learning products and activities that honor her learning style, for math, science, history, reading, etc.

- *7 Kinds of Smart Revised and Updated with Information on 2 New Kinds of Smart* by Thomas Armstrong, Ph.D.
- *Coloring Outside the Lines: Raising a Smarter Kid by Breaking All the Rules* by Roger Schank
- *In Their Own Way: Discovering and Encouraging Your Child's Multiple Intelligences,* revised and updated by Thomas Armstrong, Ph.D.
- *How Children Learn* by John Holt
- *Rich Kid, Smart Kid: Giving Your Child a Financial Head Start* by Robert Kiyosaki and Sharon Lechter
- *The Creative Spirit* by Daniel Goleman, Paul Kaufman, and Michael Ray
- *The Hurried Child: Growing Up Too Fast Too Soon* by James Elkind
- *The Myth of the A.D.D. Child* by Thomas Armstrong, Ph.D.

IDENTIFYING AND NURTURING YOUR CHILD'S MULTIPLE INTELLIGENCES

As mentioned in Chapter One, Harvard University psychologist Howard Gardner identified seven different intelligences in his 1983 book, *Frames of Mind: The Theory of Multiple Intelligences* (and his refined theory of an eighth intelligence in 1996). In this book, Gardner explains the importance of valuing skills and talents outside those that have been traditionally used to judge the merit of one's knowledge or intelligence. *The Theory of Multiple Intelligences* provides a framework for parents to help their children reach their maximum potential, utilizing their natural talents as a foundation to broaden their experiences and expand their knowledge. *The Theory of Multiple Intelligences* can be applied in a homeschool setting, but it is difficult, if not almost impossible, to apply in a traditional classroom setting. Homeschoolers have the time, resources, and ability to embrace and value their child's uniqueness and their myriad of intelligences.

Simply put, intelligence is what your child knows. Intelligence changes and adapts over time. Intelligences are not set; if they were, it would mean that we could not gain additional knowledge of any kind during our lifetime. Intelligences are not completely separate pieces of information, but rather part of a large intellect that is within each of us. According to Gardner, we all access these eight types of intelligence in our everyday learning experiences but generally one or more of these will dominate as we develop competency.

Your child might have a natural talent in one, two, or three intelligences. No one intelligence is considered superior to any other. However, some experts believe that having strong intrapersonal intelligence (also called self-smart intelligence), can greatly influence a child's future success. It is important to encourage areas of intelligence that come naturally to your child, but also build up their intelligence in an area that is not as strong. Following are the descriptions of each type of intelligence. As you read through them, resist the temptation to categorize your child into one of the eight intelligence groups. Your child is much more complex than this. Facilitate intelligence in all eight areas, using the activities listed in each intelligence as your guide. Take care that the learning materials and activities you use to increase their intelligence is in their learning style. For example, if your child has a weakness in verbal-linguistic intelligence, and their learning style is kinesthetic, you could encourage them to read books about building rockets, clay figures, or whatever their interests are, and then have them use their natural learning style to build the item they read about. Also, you could have them build a science experiment and then put on a presentation for the entire family, explaining each step that they took during the experiment's process. Use the information about intelligences to help your child develop her competency in the areas in which she is truly gifted.

The eight different intelligences are:

(1) **Verbal-Linguistic:** This intelligence is how human beings communicate and gather information. Our current schools place a high value on this intelligence. Parents can help develop their child's verbal-linguistic intelligence by reading aloud to him often, encouraging him to keep a diary, and by encouraging him to tell stories and jokes. Society will judge your child's overall intelligence based on his verbal skills. If your child is shy, help him develop good communication skills. Help him find a new subject or area he is interested in and encourage him to tell you all about it and why he is so excited about it.

(2) **Logical-Mathematical:** This is another intelligence that is recognized in schools. This intelligence allows us to think in sequences, process logical concepts, and problem solve. Mathematicians and engineers are often gifted in this intelligence. Help your child see patterns in everyday life. Use mathematical brainteasers and puzzles and the concept of money to encourage this intelligence in your child.

(3) **Spatial:** This intelligence is one that artists, designers, city planners, developers, and architects have in abundance. This intelligence allows us to think in images and pictures. The ability to see the final product (even before it is finished) is important and a good skill to have. Encourage your child to draw often and create art in many different forms. Have her look at a detailed picture and then close the book and have her describe it to you. Have her draw her dream house or bedroom. Ask her where she would put the bed, dresser, and toys in this dream bedroom.

(4) **Physical/Kinesthetic:** World-class athletes usually are very gifted in this intelligence. But all children need to develop their kinesthetic/physical intelligence. A healthy body, strength, and the mind-body connection depend on development of this intelligence. Encourage your child to dance, role-play, do plays for your family, and participate in individual or team sports that she is interested in.

(5) **Musical:** Mozart and Beethoven had large amounts of this intelligence. Encourage your child to hum, sing, or whistle. Have him learn how to

play an instrument of his choice. Play music often in the house and expose your child to community concerts and talented musicians, especially if no one in your family plays an instrument.

(6) **Intrapersonal:** This intelligence is often called the "self-smart" intelligence. Individuals with strong intrapersonal intelligence seem to have an inner wisdom. They know themselves instinctively. Self-esteem and a strong sense of self go hand-in-hand with this intelligence. Encourage your child to spend time alone daydreaming and to respect their inner thoughts and intuition in all situations.

(7) **Interpersonal:** Individuals that have good people skills are often gifted in this intelligence. They are often charismatic and can communicate well with others. Even if you think sales or politics are not going to be part of your child's future, this intelligence needs to be developed and is critical to her future success. Encourage her from time to time to put herself in another's shoes. What would be the best way to reach that person? Motivate that person? Help your child nurture her ability to sense others' motives. Help her feel empathy for others and encourage her to be a good listener. This intelligence will go a long way to helping her build strong and fulfilling relationships with family and friends.

(8) **Naturalist:** Almost all children are born with a strong naturalist intelligence. They are drawn to animals and nature. Veterinarians often are gifted in this intelligence as are scientists and explorers. As your children get older, keep their naturalist intelligence alive by planning lots of outdoor activities, field trips to nature centers, and exposure to all types of animals and plants. Encourage their interest in thunder and rainbows, and other areas of earth science.

An understanding of these areas of intelligence allows you to spot your child's natural areas of competence. Identifying those natural inclinations gives your child the opportunity to explore them slowly and build a sense of competence, which may later develop into an expertise that may one day lead to greatness.

DISCOVERING YOUR CHILD'S NATURAL INSTINCTS

Kathy Kolbe was selected by *Time* magazine in 1985 as one of seven American "new pioneers" and was named by the White House as one of the fifty Americans with a "can do" spirit. She works with major corporations as a team-building consultant and also authored two books, *The Conative Connection* and *Pure Instinct*. Kathy developed an index for children (ages thirteen and over) that can determine a child's natural instinct. Kathy believes that genius lies in a person's natural instincts. The Kolbe Y index is a tool that can help you obtain a better understanding of your role in nurturing your child's natural talents. There is an adult index available as well at www.homeschool.com/kolbe.

ALLOW YOUR CHILD TO "SAMPLE" DIFFERENT INTERESTS

While this might seem easier to apply to your homeschooling than learning styles or intelligences, there is a catch: You have to let your child quit. Yes, you have to let her quit piano after only two months if she decides piano is not for her. (She may come back to it later.) Mariah wanted to learn to dance when she was three. So her parents enrolled in a creative movement class one day a week. Within a few months it became a struggle to get Mariah to put on her tights for the thirty-minute dance class. Mariah's parents let her quit. She did not want to put on the tights and decided she was done with dance. At six, Mariah begged to try dance again, so her parents purchased all the pricey gear required and signed her back up. Mariah has continued to dance for twelve years to rave reviews, and has decided to make dance her life's work.

Children have to sample many different things in life so that first "spark" of interest in something can ignite. They are building up a library of what the world has to offer. If they are stuck in piano, they might never have a chance to discover they have a special talent in guitar, drums, or singing. As a parent, you have to be your child's "interest advocate." And this is going to be hard. You have to stand up to other adults and maybe even grandparents that think you are raising a quitter. Your children are not quitters, they're explorers. Give them this special time in life to explore what they find interesting. Often one pursuit lends itself to another but is not easily apparent to the parent. This was the case for Adam.

Adam was a fairly typical young boy who loved science—everything from frogs to rockets. He was always particularly good at math and seemed to be heading down a track that would lead him into some kind of math- or science-oriented career. At age thirteen, just by chance, Adam picked up a guitar. Much to everyone's surprise, Adam seemed to have a natural talent. His parents allowed him to put aside his traditional math and science studies, even though he seemed to be on the fast track to an early science and math career, and let him immerse himself in this newly found talent. Over the next two years, Adam made the brilliant correlation between math and music theory and intensely began to experiment with charting music by hand and playing other instruments like the trombone and piano. He dove deep into music history and listened to every type of music he could get his hands on. He began to play his original guitar compositions in public and at age fifteen was invited by an acclaimed international guitarist to participate in a ten-day guitar seminar in France.

When a child is allowed to pursue an interest, the learning and wisdom they will gain from that experience will far exceed the brief embarrassment you felt telling the piano teacher your child wasn't coming back.

THERE ARE NO "GIFTED" OR "SPECIAL NEEDS" STUDENTS

"In 30 years of teaching kids, rich and poor, I almost never met a learning disabled child; hardly ever met a gifted and talented one either. Like all school categories, these are sacred myths, created by human imagination. They derive from questionable values we never examine because they preserve the temple of schooling."

John Taylor Gatto, former New York "Teacher of the Year,"
The Underground History of American Education

While some children do have "real" physical, emotional, or brain impairments and need an education that is customized for their particular needs, hundreds of thousands of other children in schools are being labeled as "special needs" simply because their learning style and intelligences are not honored in the classroom. According to Thomas Armstrong, Ph.D., author of *In Their Own Way: Discovering and Encouraging Your Child's Multiple Intelligences:*

> It's time for the schools, and parents as well, to start focusing their attention on the inner capabilities of each and every child. We've known for years that human beings use only a small fraction of their potential. Yet schools persist in labeling hundreds of thousands of children with perfectly normal brains as attention deficit disordered or learning disabled when in fact teachers simply have not found a way of teaching them on their own terms, according to their own unique patterns of neurological functioning.

Our current school system does not always acknowledge how each child learns best. If a child learns while listening to someone lecture, while reading material from a board or in a textbook, or by doing worksheets, and is "smart" in the two intelligences schools value—mathematical and verbal-linguistic—they will most likely do well in school. But what of the vast majority of our nation's forty-eight million school-age children who learn differently? Schools have a hard time accommodating different learning styles, but they are quick to label a child as having "learning differences." What happens to these children?

Remember Joanne from Chapter One? Joanne will most likely be treated like hundreds of thousands of other children who learn differently from what schools consider normal. She will be identified as having a problem. She will be forced to endure endless hours of testing to identify her "problem." Most likely, she will be diagnosed with attention deficit disorder, a learning disability, hyperactivity, or a reading disability. She will be relegated to special education located in a portable classroom where her specially trained teacher will try to fix her "problem" with all the latest methods, special materials, and perhaps medication.* What is Joanne's real problem? School. School is boring. Joanne is a kinesthetic learner and does not learn well when her teacher lectures. She does not like reading textbooks and hates sitting all day in a desk.

> "How many thinkers and creative spirits are wasted, how much brain power goes down the drain because of our archaic, insular notions of brain and education? The numbers are undoubtedly horrendous."
>
> Jean Houston, *The Possible Human*

Robert Kiyosaki, author of four best-selling books, including his latest, *Rich Kid, Smart Kid,* says:

Today I would be labeled as having attention deficit disorder (ADD) and would probably be drugged to keep me in my seat and force me to study subjects I was not interested in. When people ask me what ADD is or wonder if they have it, I tell them that many of us have it. If we did not have it, there would be only one television channel and we would all sit there and watch it mindlessly. Today, ADD could also be known as channel surfing. When we get bored, we simply push the button and look for something of interest. Unfortunately, our kids do not have that luxury in school.

There are currently 2.5 million children in the United States labeled as ADD or ADHD (attention deficit hyperactivity disorder). These children are often treated with medication. The medication most often prescribed is Ritalin, and its use by school-age children has risen 700 percent in the last eight years.[†] What does

---

In Their Own Way: Discovering and Encouraging Your Child's Multiple Intelligences by Thomas Armstrong, Ph.D. (J. P. Tarcher, 2000), p. 11.
[†]Ibid., p. 8.

all this Ritalin use mean for society? Are we raising a generation of children who will grow up believing that they need medication in order to function in daily life? The physical side effects of Ritalin can include nausea, headaches, increased colds and influenza, and general fatigue. Not to mention that some physicians believe Ritalin can be addictive.* But what of the damage to a child's self-esteem? What effect will these 2.5 million children—children who were drugged throughout their early years—have on our society?

Children who were labeled ADD in school, and were taking Ritalin, are often able to stop taking the drug after they have been homeschooled for a time. For children with short attention spans, who learn by touch, and need freedom to move around while learning, homeschooling is a great fit for them. Also, when a child's internal clock is considered before they are presented with learning activities or encouraged to acquire a new skill, the likelihood of them being diagnosed with a learning disorder is small. All children have an internal "time clock." This "time clock" is described perfectly by homeschooling parent Le Ann Burchfield in *The First Year of Homeschooling Your Child*:

> In order for a child to learn certain things, something needs to be turned on neurologically. Each child has a built-in time clock for this to occur, and nothing can be done externally to turn it on any earlier. You can try to teach a three-month-old baby to walk, but you will face only frustration until the baby is neurologically ready to walk. It works the same way with reading, writing, bike riding—just about any skill.

Homeschooling allows parents to look for their child's "readiness" in all learning endeavors. Homeschoolers who learn to read at nine, ten, or eleven (late by school standards, but right according to the child's own developmental clock), have the wonderful advantage of not being labeled as having a "reading disability."

When children first start writing letters and numbers, they often reverse them.

End Your Addiction Now by Charles Gant and G. Lewis (Warner, 2002).

They write a B backward or the number 9 backward. You can show them how to write it the "right" way, and five minutes later they write it backward again. This very well may be developmental. One day a child is doing it the wrong way and the next day he's doing it the right way. But in school, if children continue to reverse their letters or numbers past the age that schools have deemed "unacceptable," the child can suddenly be looked at as having a learning disability.

Often parents who take their learning disabled child out of school notice something amazing after a few short months. Their child's learning disability disappears. Of course, not every child's learning disability will disappear if she is removed from school. She can have a real learning disability that is not school induced. If your child has special needs, you will have to spend a fair amount of time developing a customized plan for her education at home. But it can be done. There is a great deal of support for the parent homeschooling a special needs child. In the Resource Guide, you will find a list of Web sites, e-lists, and educational companies that offer products for special needs education at home. The Internet can also be a great tool for the special needs child. Physically disabled homeschoolers can take online elementary, high school, and college classes at home, from some of the finest universities in the world. According to Carol Hughes, parent advocate for Georgia Tech's Center for Rehabilitation Technology, "When you're on the Internet, in a chat room, or taking an online class, your disability is invisible and irrelevant. You're on equal footing."

HOMESCHOOLING AND THE "SPECIAL NEEDS" CHILD

"Ted never did well in school—not even in the special programs and schools in which they enrolled him. He was diagnosed with ADHD when he was six, and given Ritalin and other drugs. He spent much of his childhood drugged. And he continued to flounder educationally. When he was in eighth grade, he was in an ESE school that was for children who had learning disabilities and emotional problems. Many of these kids were violent and uncontrollable, and it was not easy for my gentle son. I became increasingly worried about Ted, as he became more and more depressed and not doing anything at all academically. I begged my ex to allow me to homeschool Ted. I knew that Ted was very intelligent and loved to learn, but that he just wasn't being taught the way he was able to learn. It took a long time, but about two years ago, Ted was sent to my home in North Florida. At first he was almost afraid to try to do schoolwork, but we did most of our work on the computer, and I got a special teacher's program that allowed me to make up his tests. This was very helpful for Ted, because like a lot of ADD kids, he has dysgraphia, and writing is very difficult for him. Once I formatted all his quizzes and tests into multiple choice and true and false, he had no problems. I allowed Ted to study things he wanted to know about, like history. I got cable, and made sure we got Discovery and the History Channel.

Sometimes it seemed to me that I wasn't teaching him at all. But to my astonishment, he went from a third-grade math ability to a ninth-grade one in less than three months. And when he had his first annual evaluation, he passed to the ninth grade without any problem at all. My only regret is that I did not get to homeschool Ted when he was a child, before he was traumatized by the public school system. So many times, I heard his father or grandparents say, 'What's going to happen to poor little Teddie?' And now Ted is showing that he is just as gifted as his sisters. He amazes even me! He now has more confidence also. And he has discovered abilities he never knew he had."

Chylene—North Florida

All children are gifted. Gifted is a term that schools use to label children who are gifted in verbal-linguistic and mathematical intelligences. What of the child who has a natural talent in intrapersonal or musical intelligence? Aren't they gifted too? "Gifted" is a school term. "Special needs" is a school term. If your child has an exceptional ability in verbal-linguistic intelligence, like homeschooler Sean Conley, winner of the 2001 National Spelling Bee, homeschooling allows you to look for innovative ways to encourage this intelligence in your child. Your child can read college-level books, take online college classes, or work in the community, helping adults to learn to read. He or she does not have to stay at their grade level in reading or spelling. Grade level is irrelevant at home. If your thirteen-year-old has an enormous talent in math and wants to build a computer, no problem. As a homeschooling parent, you have the freedom to explore different options for making this happen for your child. Teachers don't have the time or resources to assist your child in developing his special areas of interest. Homeschooling parents have far more flexibility and resources to develop a project that supports a child's special talents and interests. You can find a mentor in the community for your child to work with to build a computer, or you might consider asking a family member to build the computer with your child. Regardless of your challenges, remember that every child is gifted. Honor her unique learning style and her intelligences. Your child is a talented and unique child who has special needs—just like every other child. Honor the individual in your child. Honor how he learns best, his passions and talents. If you don't, how will your child ever learn to honor himself?

CHAPTER EIGHT

Homeschooling and the Working Parent

As you read this book, you will hopefully get a good feel for all the many advantages to homeschooling your child. But like anything, there are disadvantages. Other than small issues like a perpetually messy house, disapproving family members, or a little less time to just be by yourself, there is one very big disadvantage that many families face—loss of income.

At a time in America when it can be difficult for a family to live on two incomes, living on one or one and a half can be especially challenging. For some homeschooling families, one spouse has a well-paying job and money is not an issue. Other families have a very frugal lifestyle and can live well on one income. But for the vast majority of homeschooling families, the loss of a second income, or the possibility of living on one income for many years, can make it hard for them to even consider homeschooling.

But if you believe homeschooling is the best choice for your family, there is good news. Homeschooling parents across the country, regardless of their educational background, location, or job history, have found ways to supplement their spouse's income, replace a second income, or not give up any income at all. And some families have taken a detailed look at how their family was spending money and adjusted their lifestyle to allow them to live on less income, often without feeling any great sacrifice.

While you explore different options for making sure your family's financial needs are met, keep in mind that whatever you decide, simply taking this time to reexamine your family's lifestyle choices will be beneficial. And if you are able to create a telecommuting position, arrange to job "shift" with your spouse, or start a home-based business, the rewards will be twofold—you are making sure that your family's financial needs are taken care of and your children will see that you consider spending time with them more important than anything else in the world.

HOW DO YOU EARN MONEY AND HOMESCHOOL TOO?

"I work only two days a week and my mother, who recently retired, was a willing participant in our homeschooling. My husband arrives home around one p.m. and teaches afternoon topics. So you could say our son has a three to one teacher-to-student ratio."

Julia—Battle Creek, Michigan

"How I'd envy parents who could be at home and get to be involved. I remember telling my husband that we couldn't do this because of finances. I am a registered nurse and my husband commutes to work one and a half hours from our home each day. With lots of prayers and advice from educators, we went out on a limb and began homeschooling this past August. Thanks to the mentorship of a Christian curriculum program, our daughter is painting her own sky and reaching for the stars! We get excited watching her enthusiasm and love for education. She now studies without the stresses of a classroom. I am fortunate to schedule my two hospital shifts around her classroom time. Her dad teaches math and flute in the afternoons. Our family has the best of both worlds! A special favorite is the scheduled field trips and dining out at lunchtime each day. If we had known that homeschooling was this fulfilling, we would have made the plunge years ago!"

Bruce and Shawn M.

LIVING ON ONE INCOME IN A TWO-INCOME WORLD

You do not have to live in a tent in order to homeschool your children. Being home with your child is considered a luxury today, but many homeschoolers have found that having one person home full-time has actually simplified and improved their lives. If you want to homeschool your children but think you can't afford it, you're in for a wonderful surprise. Judith Waite Allee, coauthor of *Homeschooling on a Shoestring*, believes that:

If you don't think you can afford to homeschool because you need your job, you have some options. They boil down to earning more or spending less. We did a combination of the two. My husband is a freelance photographer with a home-based business. That allowed us both to be home with our kids until the youngest was nine years old. Then I got a part-time job, and later a full-time job, and he was the full-time at-home parent. I won't say there weren't any sacrifices financially, or that we were all that smart about it, but then, sending your child to daycare or to school may be a bigger sacrifice—it's just not a financial one. Cutting back your expenses could make the difference between needing to work and being home with your family. Try a pencil and paper comparison of all your work-related expenses—childcare, lunches out, work clothes, dry cleaning, and transportation. You might be surprised. Be sure to look at the bottom-line difference on your taxes. Does your job put you in a different tax bracket? Would you be able to live more thriftily—with more time for yard sales and comparison shopping—if you were home? My youngest will be twenty-one tomorrow. It makes me think back. I don't believe for a minute her childhood memories are any less rich because of our financial sacrifices. On the other hand, I think our learning together and having time together made a big difference in our lives. I hope our thrifty ways passed on an important value to my children. They saw us reusing and repairing things and they know we're helping the environment. They know that tomatoes don't grow in plastic wrap, and that a fresh garden tomato is a true luxury, and it's cheaper as well. Being frugal doesn't mean you have to wash your plastic Baggies or turn your dryer lint into a Cinderella Halloween costume. It simply means that you spend your money on things that are important to you and don't spend it on things that don't give you that much pleasure. If buying a new sofa means that you have to work away from your family for 40 hours, then you may decide that it's not worth it. However, you may decide that a family vacation *would* be well worth those 40 hours.

RESOURCES FOR FRUGAL LIVING

- *Home Schooling on a Shoestring* by Melissa Morgan and Judith Waite Allee
- *Home Schooling from Scratch: Simple Living—Super Learning* by Mary Potter Kenyon
- *Your Money or Your Life: Transforming Your Relationship with Money and Achieving Financial Independence* by Joe Dominguez and Vicki Robin
- *Getting a Life: Strategies for Simple Living, Based on the Revolutionary Program for Financial Freedom, Your Money or Your Life* by Jacqueline Blix and David Heitmiller
- *The Average Family's Guide to Financial Freedom* by Bill and Mary Toohney

Many homeschoolers report that a streamlined lifestyle actually feels richer—lives are less cluttered and children appreciate what they have. Homeschooling parents Patricia and Doug purchased a much smaller home in an older neighborhood. The difference in mortgage payments, area of house to clean, and slower pace of the neighborhood actually enhanced their homeschooling lifestyle. Penny, another homeschooler, buys no curriculum. Instead, she makes up her own, following the interests and readiness of the children. Sometimes the children prepare their own lessons. Meanwhile, Sarah stays away from toy stores. The children craft their own very creative and fun toys (e.g., a flat box with taped-in sections becomes a cash register). Maggie is an unschooler and literally never spends any money on homeschooling. Life is their classroom, nature is their constant source of discovery, harmonizing relationships is social studies, helping Grandma once a week is their community service, music and art is their opportunity for creativity, and being together as a family is their joy.

If you are working, you may want to run the numbers. Your job may not be bringing in as much as you think. Many homeschoolers find that when they quit work, their expenses drop dramatically since they no longer have those sneaky work-related expenses like dry cleaning, lunches out, gas, day care, and higher taxes. By the time you subtract the true costs of working from your paycheck, you may find that your job is not adding that much to your family's finances.

Deciding to homeschool may cause you to reevaluate what's important to you. If you're still not sure whether or not you want to keep your job, you may want to do the exercise suggested in the book *Homeschooling on a Shoestring*. Simply fold a piece of paper in half so that it forms two columns. Label the left column "Reasons to Keep My Job" and label the right column "Reasons to Quit My Job." Putting it all down on paper may help you and your spouse decide what's best for your family.

Remember, it is not necessary for you to quit your job and stay at home full-time in order to homeschool your children. It's your choice. And it's nice to know that you can earn money and still be with your children.

WORKING FROM HOME

Although it is possible to live on one income, many homeschoolers choose to work and homeschool at the same time. Working from home is a natural fit for homeschoolers. It allows you to earn money and still be with your children. In California, William works for a large company that sells medical supplies. William makes sales calls three days a week and works from his home office the other two days. "Although I don't directly help teach the kids as much as my wife does, my being home is a big help. Because I'm home during the kids' naptime, my wife can slip out to run errands or exercise without having to hire a baby-sitter. Plus, because I can see what the kids are doing, I'm less prone to those 'Are they learning anything?' fears that sometimes plague other homeschooling dads."

For us, using technology effectively has enabled us to work from a home office and still run a company. We both use cell phones, Palms, laptops, and fax machines to stay in touch with other Homeschool.com team members in California and in Virginia, who also work virtually from a home office. We also outsource some of our company's business needs to outside vendors, which eliminates the need for a large corporate office. Using technology to work from home is an option for everyone, either in your own home-based business or as a telecommuting employee.

WORK-AT-HOME RESOURCES

- *The Stay-at-Home Mom's Guide to Making Money* by Liz Folger
- *Home Business, Big Business* by Mel Cook
- *Working from Home* by Paul and Sarah Edwards
- *Mompreneurs: A Mother's Practical Step-by-Step Guide to Work-at-Home Success* by Ellen Parlapiano and Patricia Cole
- *The Work-at-Home Mom's Guide to Home Business* by Cheryl Demas

Telecommuting is becoming increasingly popular. According to Online Moms.com: "In 1990 there were 4 million telecommuters. By the late 1990s, that number grew to 11 million, and according to Find/SVP, there will be 14 million telecommuters by the early 2000s." Technology is a major reason for this growth. The availability and affordability of computers, fax machines, and the Internet has made it easier for millions of Americans to work from their homes.

Alesia is a teacher who never uses a classroom. She is an educational specialist for a charter school in California. She takes her children with her when she visits other homeschooling families and uses her laptop to record the students' learning records. She also does all of her ordering of educational products, reports, and communications electronically. Alesia not only earns a second income for her family, she gets to work with other homeschooling families and her children get a chance to make new friends.

Some jobs are more readily adapted to telecommuting than others and work that can be done using a computer, a modem, or a fax machine are the best candidates. Sales jobs and work that requires extensive telephone use can be done from home. For example, writing, proofreading, word processing, Web design, and graphic design jobs are all easily done from a home office.

The advantage of working from your home is that you will have more flexibility and more time with your kids. However, unless your children are serious unschoolers, you will probably need someone to look after the younger ones while you work. This is especially true for formal telecommuting arrangements where you are an employee. The advantage of this situation is that although you still have a baby-sitter, you are nearby and know that your children are safe. If you are currently employed but want to start working out of your home, you can approach your employer and explain to him or her how such an arrangement would benefit the company. If your current employer is not open to telecommuting and if you are not able to find a new telecommuting job, you may still be able to telework. Teleworkers are self-employed consultants who work on projects out of their home. For example, writing business plans for companies or putting together catalogues for different companies are just two examples of telework.

Of course working at home and telecommuting are not the only family-friendly employment options available to parents today. According to Diane Keith, the editor of *Homefires* magazine: "To work and still homeschool you have to think outside the box. You also have to help others to think outside the box. Show them the advantages to letting you have flexibility in work hours. Don't rely just on what you were trained to do or your past employment history. There are a myriad other options available for those who are creative and willing to broaden their definition of 'work.'"

PART-TIME WORK

There are lots of different types of part-time work. Whether the work is done from home or away from home, most homeschoolers who work part-time are looking for a little extra income. For some homeschoolers, part-time work means working four hours a day, five days a week. For others, it may mean working nights or weekends. Tammy, a homeschooler in Los Angeles, created a part-time job where she picks up children from school in the afternoon and watches them at her house until their parents finish work.

Another homeschooler created a part-time dog grooming business. Another mom got a job as a baby-sitter in a gym. She brings her children with her and they get to play with the other children while she earns money. Michelle, a homeschooling mother in Texas, solved her homeschooling and daycare challenges by teaming up with four other mothers. These women take turns and one mom homeschools the children in the morning while the other moms go to work at outside jobs. This allows each mom to work part-time four days a week.

Part-time work offers several advantages. You can continue to earn an income and still have time for your family, your friends, and for yourself. As one homeschooling mom puts it: "Even if I didn't homeschool my children, I would never want to work full-time again. When I quit my very full-time job and went down to work part-time, I felt like I had gotten my life back." And since part-time work has been around for a long time (unlike telecommuting and job sharing), you can cut back your hours without being relegated to the "mommy track." Women on the "mommy track" can find themselves skipped over for important promotions because their employers believe the commitment to family means they cannot be dedicated to an outside job.

Sometimes both parents will choose to work part-time in order to share in the homeschooling duties and in the finances. Sam and Cathy Williams both wanted to work and both wanted to homeschool their children, so they devised a situation where they could both work part-time. Sam works part-time as a nurse and Cathy works as a part-time English teacher. Cathy says, "This way we both get to have the pleasure of participating fully in our children's lives, while at the same time pursuing our professional goals." Another homeschooling mom works as a receptionist/bookkeeper. Her husband is a gardener. He gets home at three P.M. and she goes to work from four to seven. In addition to job "shifting" with her husband, this mom job "shares" with another homeschooling mom so that her bookkeeping job covers the required six days a week. In order to make sure they have time together as a family and as a couple, the family eats a late dinner together every evening and husband and wife go out on a "date" one night every other weekend.

JOB SHARING

Job sharing is a work situation where two people share one full-time job. Although not as common as part-time work, job sharing is gaining in popularity and has some distinct advantages. The biggest advantage is that even if you are away from the office, work gets done and questions get answered. Job sharing is a good option for those in high-level jobs who want to cut back but their job demands full-time attention. In some cases, even senior level positions can be filled by two part-time employees. And where part-time workers usually receive lower salaries, job sharers tend to enjoy higher salaries, and benefits are either continued in full for each employee or prorated to match the amount of time on the job.

Companies benefit from job sharing arrangements because there is virtually no downtime for illness or holidays and the company has coverage five days a week, fifty-two weeks a year. A single person could never give the company that kind of coverage. The down side is that some employers are reluctant to try job sharing because they worry that the employees might not get along or that one employee will be weaker than the other.

If you are interested in creating a job sharing arrangement, ask around and look for a potential job share partner. When you are considering someone, remember that communication is key to a successful job share, along with trust, common goals, and complementary strengths.

STARTING A HOME-BASED BUSINESS

Home-based businesses are particularly popular with homeschoolers since they give parents a lot of time with their children, along with the satisfaction of allowing their children to work with them in the business. Jane Williams, publisher of the Bluestocking Press catalogue, says, "My business grew as my children grew. As my children grew older, it allowed me to do more. It also taught them real life skills in the business world. After being in business for over ten years now, my daughter answers the phone and takes orders and my mother does all the bookkeeping." Mark and Helen Hegener successfully homeschooled their children while working almost full-time on their magazine *Home Education Magazine*. "It wasn't always easy, but it was always satisfying," says Helen. "When times got stressful, our children would mutter, 'It must be deadline time.' But when we asked the kids what they liked best about their childhood, one of the things they said they liked was being on the cover of the magazine and reading articles about themselves."

Raymond and Dorothy Moore, considered by many to be the grandparents of the homeschooling movement, believe that home industries help children develop self-respect in a way that no other activity can match. They believe that manual work unites and balances head and hand and that it nurtures creativity. Their book, *Minding Your Own Business,* offers practical advice on how to bring children into home management and home industries and offers almost five hundred examples of home businesses and services. According to the Moores:

> The one method most likely to help parents avoid burnout in home teaching is to allow at least half the day for activities in which children can work constructively and creatively, usually with you, but with increased responsibility as they mature and can accept commensurate authority. Don't worry if your children are only six or eight years old. Make them the officers in your family "corporation." Let your oldest or most able be your president; but you had better be chairman of the board. By the time they can handle math, let them run your checking account to pay family bills; the bank then will correct their "papers," or they will correct the bank. Propose that all they save over the year in family expenses, you will split with them at year's end.

The second income from a home-based business can be larger than working a job outside the home because of the expenses that are saved from not working outside the home, and tax benefits. Childcare, even part-time, can take a big chunk out of a family's income. If your children are not toddlers, you don't necessarily need a baby-sitter while you work. Homeschooling children are very self-directed learners and can do their learning right alongside you as you work. A work wardrobe is often unnecessary, given that one or two nice outfits should meet your needs if you occasionally have a meeting outside your home office. Transportation costs should be less, since you are not commuting to work each day. Also, equipment, product, and automotive expenses that your business incurs can be deducted on your tax returns (Schedule C and related schedules for identifying business expenses). Make sure to follow the IRS guidelines. Depending on your business, many products, such as computers and desks, can be used on a limited basis for personal use. Also, some home-based businesses can deduct a portion of the utilities, homeowners insurance, and home maintenance based on their square footage of their home office. Again, be diligent in knowing what business models qualify for a home-office deduction, and seek help from a CPA if you are unsure.

Some homeschooling parents, like Cheryl Demas, started a home-based business that has become very successful and has provided them with both financial and personal gains.

In 1994, in the space of a few weeks, Cheryl delivered her second child and discovered that her seven-year-old had diabetes. She felt that her children needed her home. So she quit her job and began homeschooling her older daughter. But in Cheryl's mind staying at home did not mean giving up a career that had included eleven years working at Honeywell and Cable Data and a degree in mathematics and computer science.

Intent on finding a way to put her skills as a software engineer to work, Cheryl began surfing the Internet for opportunities. After wading through the work-at-home scams and schemes, Cheryl launched a Web site design business but was simultaneously drawn to establish a site where she could post her thoughts about starting a home-based business.

"I wrote about my home business experiences and the transition from being a working mom to a homeschooling at-home mom," Cheryl says. "I soon heard from women from all over the world who were in the same boat, women who wanted to be home with their kids but wanted to work and make money too." WAHM (Work-At-Home Moms) was off to a great start.

Run from her home in Folsom, California, WAHM.com receives more than two million hits per month and, with advertiser support, makes money. And users aren't the only ones giving WAHM.com recognition. The Go Network gave WAHM.com its best three-star rating, one of only sixteen women's sites to receive such a rating. *USA Today* featured it as a hot site of the day, and *Better Homes & Gardens* remarked: "Mothering is working at home, of course, but WAHM.com is for women holding down two jobs: as a parent and as a stay-at-home breadwinner."

SINGLE-PARENT HOMESCHOOLING

Single-parent homeschooling is being done, and done well. Take Victoria Moran, for example. When her husband died unexpectedly, she knew she had to get out and earn a living, but she worried about being away from her daughter at a time when they really needed to be together. Victoria had always wanted to write and speak, so she wrote a book and traveled around the world with her daughter, making speeches. Her book is called *Shelter for the Spirit*. According to Victoria, "My daughter does her studies at the dining room table while I work on the computer. Once, when I was being interviewed on a radio show, I looked through the glass and saw her chatting with Isaac Asimov! It's been such a comfort to me to know that I can provide for my family—without leaving my daughter behind."

Single-parent homeschooling takes creativity and help. Some homeschoolers have been lucky enough to find a workplace that welcomes children, some trade off schooling and childcare with other homeschooling families. As children grow older and more independent, childcare becomes less necessary and homeschooling becomes easier.

Sandra homeschools her eleven-year-old half the day and works as a real estate agent the other half. "In real estate, a great deal of flexibility is required. When things are slow, my daughter and I take a trip or do some fun educational projects together. But when times are busier and I'm in the middle of a sale, my daughter spends time reading while I'm at my appointments, or plays at a friend's house. As a single mom, homeschooling has meant a lot to us because it's allowed us to grab all the time together we can."

Homeschooling doesn't have to take eight hours a day. Much of the time spent in the classroom is filled with busywork, and out of the six hours spent in school, probably only three are spent on academics. You can homeschool your child for two to four hours a day and still have time to work. The key to successful single-parent homeschooling is to let your children know that you can't be parent, educator, and household manager without their help.

Thousands of homeschooling parents, from all walks of life, are able to earn the money they need—and still homeschool their children. You can too! Don't let concerns about money stop you from having this incredible experience with your children. With a little creative thought, you too will be able to get the money you need—with your children at your side.

CHAPTER NINE

Click Learning:
Homeschooling on the Internet

THE INTERNET OFFERS UNLIMITED POSSIBILITIES FOR children to use the entire world as their classroom. In this, the information age, learning is no longer confined to four walls and textbooks. With the world at their fingertips, children have the opportunity to learn from the finest teachers and resources in the world. For example, they can explore alongside world-famous scientists like Dr. Robert Ballard, work to save endangered species with international environmentalists, and communicate virtually with children from all over the world with the click of a mouse.

With new forms of communication coming into play at lightning speed, knowledge has fewer and fewer boundaries.

RECOMMENDED READING

- *Homeschool Your Child for Free: More Than 1,200 Smart, Effective, and Practical Resources for Home Education on the Internet and Beyond* by Laura Maery Gold and Joan Zielinski
- *The Parent's Guide to Protecting Your Children in Cyberspace* by Parry Aftab

Children who are educated to see the entire world as their classroom not only increase their potential for knowledge, but also have the advantage of realizing their role in an international culture. Homeschoolers can travel virtually to France with Homeschool.com's media team, where they can explore the lifestyles, culture, and history of their French neighbors. Or connect with other children all around the planet by sharing their hopes, dreams, and everyday life via a message board or live chat.

The Internet has made homeschooling easier than ever and may be one of the reasons homeschooling is growing more popular every day. According to Mark Hegener, founder of *Home Education Magazine:* "Homeschoolers are very well connected. In the day-to-day life of a community this diverse, the Internet allows for interaction and sharing of experiences. Also, the Internet is the biggest library there is. Because homeschoolers are less dependent on a fixed schedule of class periods, there's a lot of time for kids to follow their passion. The Internet is a great tool for this."*

THE BIGGEST LIBRARY THERE IS

It's eight P.M. and your child has just finished reading an "awesome" book about the ancient Egyptian mummification process. The book is thorough, but she wants to know if the mummification jars had a specific name, and how to write her name in hieroglyphics and . . . She is so excited and motivated and wants to learn more—now! In two minutes or less you and your historian-to-be can be searching the ancient Egyptian superhighway—the Internet.

In the fast-moving information age, children can learn about anything they are interested in at any time via the Internet—they just need to know where to look. Where do you search? How do you find the name of those ancient Egyptian mummification jars? When you know where to look, the Internet can help

*This quote from Mark Hegener originally appeared in *Access Magazine,* August 13, 2000, page 6.

you build an education for your child that is customized and individualized for their particular interests and skills.

BEST SEARCH ENGINES

#1 Google.com

#2 Yahooligans.com

#3 MetaCrawler.com

Search engines are the main entrance on to the Internet. Sadly, however, search engines are not what they used to be, and many search engines list only sites that pay to be listed. Other search engines give you so many results, you can spend hours looking for the information you want. Homeschool.com tested search engines by searching for the words "Egyptian mummification jars" and analyzing the results. The top three search engines were: Google, Yahooligans, and MetaCrawler. Google (www.google.com) had the best results, mentioning canopic jars in the site descriptions and taking you directly to the right site. Yahooligans (www.yahooligans.com) gave a nice list of subsearches about pharaohs, Egyptian mythology and religion, the Nile River, and the pyramids. MetaCrawler (www.MetaCrawler.com) also delivered a good list of subcategories that included information on the mummification process, mummies, and Egypt. Ask Jeeves for Kids (www.ajkids.com) did well in an earlier test by Homeschool.com but did not fare well in the 2001 test, delivering no results for the question "What is the name of the Egyptian mummification jars?" and two broken links when the search words were "Egyptian." The "Study Tools" section, which is set up like a library reference desk, also included a large number of broken links. The "Tours" section of Ask Jeeves for Kids, however, is still a good resource for homeschoolers and includes fun information about wildlife, pirates, and wizardry.

Online tutors and homework helpers are popular with homeschooling families because they provide assistance and answers around the clock. Whether you need help with a pesky math or grammar problem, or if you want to learn how to build rockets, someone is always there to help you. A number of different Web sites offer tutorial services. Tutor.com is probably the best known site, providing live homework help and access to qualified instruction in an online classroom for $20 an hour. EducationPlanet.com has a free service that helps you find tutors in your area. Homeworkhelp.com, StudentAcademy.com, About.com/homework, StudyWeb.com, and EducationPlanet.com all offer free tutoring and homework help. Most of these free services do not answer children's questions directly; instead, they provide an index of topics for the students to choose from. For example, if your child gets stuck on an algebra problem, he can find minilessons on algebraic expressions, exponents, or graphing. Or he can type in that pesky math problem and watch the computer solve it. In addition to general homework sites, there are also tutoring sites for specific subjects like www.algebra-online.com or GoMath.com. With the help of a good search engine and a good homework and tutorial site, you'll be able to answer all those "why" and "how come" questions that children have.

ONLINE HOMESCHOOLING STORES

Timberdoodle Company
www.timberdoodle.com

Homeschool Central Mall
www.homeschoolcentralmall.com

The Sycamore Tree
www.sycamoretree.com

God's World Book Club
www.gwbc.com/godsworld

Homeschool Discount
www.homeschooldiscount.com

Online curriculum is becoming more and more popular because it allows children to learn at their own pace. If a child has an interest in a certain subject, she can pursue it to a Ph.D. level if she wants, no matter her age. According to a *USA Weekend* survey, 44 percent of school districts have "distance learning" programs. This means that you can use online curriculum through an independent Web site, like Homeschool.com's online curriculum for Grades K–7, or you can take online courses that are associated with an established high school or university. Either way, you and your child are still in charge of her learning. Younger homeschoolers may sign up for a year's curriculum from Homeschool.com, K12.com, or Alpha Omega Academy Online. Older homeschoolers may sign up for individual classes through an accredited online school like Keystone High School, or may take a number of free and almost-free online programs through the homework and tutoring sites described here, or from a specialty math and science site like Edventures.com. Whether your child wants to learn for learning's sake or in order to earn a diploma or college degree, online learning is a natural fit for homeschoolers.

Of course the Internet has obvious benefits, like being able to research information. There is also a hidden benefit—that the Internet is helping children become good writers. This makes sense when you consider that to communicate online, either in a chat room, on a bulletin board, or in an e-mail letter, kids have to write. It's how they "talk" online. This new generation of Internet-savvy kids also has the ability to connect with people from all over the world in a way not possible just a few years ago. Instead of writing to a pen pal and waiting weeks for a reply, today's kids can instantly trade photos and stories across the globe, learning about cultures not from a travel guide, but from the people who actually live there.

The Internet is also a great resource for parents who are struggling to find information and support for their special needs child. In the past, parents had to dig for scraps of information about their child's condition, such as the latest research, names of experts, and links to other families with the same condition. Now parents, teachers, and children who share an interest in these issues can be linked together in a way that has never happened before. The U.S. Department of Education has created an Internet clearinghouse for information on gifted children and kids with disabilities, called ERIC (www.ericec.org). LD Online (www.ldonline.com) is also recognized as one of the Web's best special needs sites, with over a million page views a month. And ADD.org (www.add.org) is a special site created for children diagnosed with attention deficit disorder and attention deficit hyperactivity disorder.

Successful parents and homeschoolers are learning that the best education is personal, and that technology is only as good as the people using it. The best ways for parents to make the most of the Internet is to learn about it and try not to be intimidated when our children know more about it than we do! Pretty soon your children will be setting their own educational goals and using the Internet to get the help and information they need.

STAYING SAFE ON THE INTERNET

Even though the good content on the Internet far outweighs the bad, families still have to learn how to use the Internet safely. Only 1 percent of the sites on the Internet are pornographic, but when Homeschool.com's team did a search for "American Girl," a pornographic site called "American Girly" came up. Although this is undesirable, it is not a threat to the child's safety. Other times, however, the Internet (particularly chat rooms) has been used to lure children into dangerous situations. There are also less obvious dangers as well. The Internet is not filtered in the same way as radio and television, which means that children are likely to see advertisements for tobacco and alcohol and to encounter hateful and racist information.

Although no one would dispute that there is a dark side to the Internet, most people are against any type of Internet regulation. This means that people must take responsibility for their own safety on the Internet and for the safety of their children. By knowing the dangers and how to avoid them, you can take advantage of all the positive aspects of the Internet while avoiding most of its pitfalls.

- Warn your children not to give out identifying information—such as a home address or telephone number—in a public message such as a chat room or bulletin board, and have your children check with you before they give this information out via e-mail. Make sure they also know not to give out any information about you or your spouse.

- Think twice before giving out sensitive financial information like credit card numbers. Make sure the company you are dealing with is reputable and processes your credit card information in a safe manner.

- Many search engines let you choose the option of having your searches filtered. Google and AOL, for example, both have features that screen out objectionable sites.

- Never respond to bulletin board messages, chat room comments, or e-mails that seem aggressive or obscene. Do not unsubscribe to these types of messages either, since that only lets the sender know that your e-mail address is still active and they can sell your address to another "spammer."

- Tell your children that if they ever feel uncomfortable with anything they encounter on the Internet or in an e-mail, they should tell you about it.

- Be very careful about arranging an in-person meeting with someone you met on the Internet. Make sure your children know that things are not always the way they appear. If you do decide to meet someone, be sure that first meeting is in a public place.

- Remind your children that just because something appears on a Web site, that doesn't necessarily make it true. Offers that are "too good to be true" probably are not genuine. Have them ask themselves, "Who wrote this material?" "What do they have to gain?" "Why should I believe them?"

- Place your computer in an area of your home that is in plain view. This will help you to keep an eye on how your child is using the computer. If your child's educational software games are too loud, you can have them use headphones.

- Work with your children to establish guidelines for computer use in your house. How much time can they spend each day? Try not to use your computer as a baby-sitter. If your child is spending too much time on the computer, if they use the computer late into the night, or if the computer has begun to take the place of real people, they may have a problem.

- Get to know your child's "online friends" the same way you would get to know their other friends.

People do outrageous things when they get behind a keyboard that they would never do in a face-to-face encounter, so make sure the entire family uses good manners on the Internet. Remind your children that the Internet is a meeting place for people from around the world, with different cultures and different ideas. In order to get along, we need to treat each other with respect and be sensitive to cultural distinctions.

The Internet has so much to offer the entire family. Once you know how to avoid the dangerous aspects of the Internet you will be able to enjoy all the positive aspects the Internet has to offer.

LET YOUR CHILDREN TEACH YOU

For most of a child's education, he is on the receiving end of the teaching and someone else always seems to know more than he does. Rarely does he have the chance to do the teaching. Computers are different. Most kids know more about computers than adults—after all, they've grown up with computers—and can outclick an adult any day. Give your child the chance to show you what he knows. Pull an extra chair up next to the computer and let your child show you around the family computer. Ask your child to show you his favorite Web sites and chat rooms. Use this opportunity to share your child's interests and get to know them even better.

If your child is young, you may want to explore a few fun sites together. Fun School.com (www.funschool.com) has a great selection of educational games for elementary school students. Games Kids Play (www.corpcomm.net/~gnieboer/gamehome.htm) has lots of old-fashioned games like Mother May I? You can also discover new sites together by clicking through Homeschool.com's list of the top 100 educational Web sites.

If your child is older or more experienced with computers, let her show you how to bookmark your favorite sites. This will give you a chance to see her bookmarks and to see what interests her. Let her show you how to use a chat room and how to attach photos and other documents to your e-mail. This will give you a chance to discuss Internet safety and to come up with some mutually agreed upon rules. The more you know about your child's computer habits, the safer you'll feel. You may even enjoy being the student for a change.

THE TOP 100 EDUCATIONAL SITES ON THE INTERNET

The Internet has changed the way we educate our children and ourselves. Adults are taking business classes online, college students are attending virtual universities, and children are following their interests and learning about the things that matter most to them. In a sense, whether you're a child, a college student, or an adult, the Internet has turned every home into a virtual homeschool.

The sites listed below represent some of the best educational sites on the Internet today. We based our selection on the following criteria:

- Is the site educational?
- Is the site well organized?
- Does the site make good use of modern Internet technology?
- Is the site interesting and informative?

After reviewing thousands of sites, the following have been selected as the top picks for 2002, containing the best educational content on the Internet today.

Art and Music

A. Pintura, Art Detective (www.eduweb.com/pintura)

Art Lessons With Talent Teacher (www.talentteacher.com)

The @rt-room (www.arts.ufl.edu/art/rt_room/)

Art Tales: Telling Stories with Wildlife Art (www.wildlifeart.org/ArtTales)

Arts Workshop (www.childrensmuseum.org/artsworkshop/index2a.html)

Children's Music Web (www.childrensmusic.org)

Inside Art (www.eduweb.com/insideart/index.html)

Kinder Art (www.kinderart.com)

Louvre W3 (http://mistral.culture.fr/louvre/louvrea.htm)

The Museum of Fine Arts, Houston (http://mfah.org/)

Webmuseum, Paris (www.oir.ucf.edu/wm/)

Fun

The Art and Craft of Movie Making (www.bbc.co.uk/education/lzone/movie/index.htm)

Coloring.com (www.coloring.com)

Cyberkids (www.cyberkids.com)

Fun Brain (www.funbrain.com)

It's Your Turn Online Games (www.itsyourturn.com)

Kids' Space (www.kids-space.org/)

Riff Interactive—Live Online Guitar Lessons (www.riffinteractive.com/Software.htm#)

World Kids Network (www.worldkids.net)

Geography and Virtual Travel

Amazon Interactive (www.eduweb.com/amazon.html)

Auto Factory Tour (www.ipl.org/autou)

Cleveland Metroparks Zoo (www.clemetzoo.com)

Colonial Williamsburg: Electronic Field Trips (www.history.org/trips)

Foreign Language For Travelers (www.travlang.com/languages)

National Geographic Society (www.nationalgeographic.com)

World Safari (www.supersurf.com)

History

America's Homepage: Plymouth, MA (www.media3.net/plymouth)

The American Civil War Homepage (http://sunsite.utk.edu/civil-war)

Ancient Egypt on the Web (http://guardians.net/egypt)

Biography.com (www.biography.com)

The Canada War Museum (www.civilization.ca/cwm/kidsection/cwmindexeng.
   html)

Castles on the Web (www.castlesontheweb.com)

The Civil War Homepage (www.civil-war.net)

The European Middle Ages (www.wsu.edu/~dee/MA/MA.HTM)

Family Search (www.familysearch.org)

History/Social Studies for K-12 Teachers (www.execpc.com/~dboals/)

Justice for Kids and Youth (www.usdoj.gov/kidspage)

K–12 Africa Guide (www.sas.upenn.edu/African_Studies/Home_Page/
   AFR_GIDE.html)

Lewis and Clark (www.pbs.org/lewisandclark)

New Perspectives on the West (www.pbs.org/weta/thewest)

The Oregon Trail (www.isu.edu/~trinmich/Oregontrail.html)

States and Capitals (www.50states.com)

WestWeb (www.library.csi.cuny.edu/westweb)

White House for Kids (www.whitehouse.gov/kids)

The World of the Vikings (www.pastforward.co.uk/vikings/index.html)

Homeschooling

About Homeschooling (www.homeschooling.about.com)

Autodidactic Press (www.autodidactic.com)

Unit Study Adventures (www.unitstudy.com)

Math

Ask Dr. Math (http://mathforum.org/dr.math/)

Basket Math Interactive (www.scienceacademy.com/BI/index.html)

Exercises in Math Readiness (http://math.usask.ca/readin/menu.html)

Math Goodies.com (www.mathgoodies.com)

Mega-Mathematics (www.c3.lanl.gov/mega-math)

Web Math (www.webmath.com)

NASA

www.nasa.gov

NASA Jet Propulsion Labratory (www.jpl.nasa.gov)

Neuroscience for Kids (http://faculty.washington.edu/chudler/neurok.html)

Ocean Planet Home Page (http://seawifs.gsfc.nasa.gov/ocean_planet.html)

Resource Center for Environmental Education (www.edu-source.com)

Searching for Extraterrestrial Intelligence (www.seti.org/game/index.html)

StarChild (http://heasarc.gsfc.nasa.gov/docs/StarChild)

St.Louis Science Center (www.slsc.org)

The Yuckiest Site on the Internet (www.yucky.kids.discovery.com)

Reading

Audrey Wood Club House (www.audreywood.com)

Bartleby.com (www.bartleby.com)

National Scrabble Association (www.scrabble-assoc.com)

Pink Monkey (www.pinkmonkey.com)

Science

Brookfield Zoo: Go Wild (www.brookfieldzoo.org)

Chem4Kids (www.chem4kids.com)

Dennis Kunkel's Microscopy (www.DennisKunkel.com)

Discovery Channel: Learning Adventures (http://school.discovery.com/school adventures)

Exploratorium (www.exploratorium.edu)

Explore Science: Interactive Science Education (www.explorescience.com)

The Franklin Institute: Learning Resources (http://sln.fi.edu/)

HowStuffWorks (www.howstuffworks.com)

Imagine the Universe! (http://imagine.gsfc.nasa.gov)

InnerBody (www.InnerBody.com)

Internet Plasma Physics Education Experience (http://ippex.pppl.gov)

Jason Project (www.jasonproject.org)

Kids Dig Reed (www.kidsdigreed.com)

Life Beyond Earth (www.pbs.org/lifebeyondearth)

The MAD Scientist Network (www.madsci.org)

Museum of Science, Boston: Online Exhibits (www.mos.org)

Writing

Crayon (http://crayon.net/)

MidLink Magazine (www.cs.ucf.edu/~MidLink/)

Researchpaper.com (www.researchpaper.com)

Take Our Word.com (www.takeourword.com)

Word Central (www.wordcentral.com)

Miscellaneous

All Experts.com (www.allexperts.com)

Babel Fish—Language Translator (http://world.altavista.com)

Britannica (www.britannica.com)

Educational Resources Information Center: ERIC (www.eric.ed.gov)

Internet Public Library (www.ipl.org)

KidsBank (www.kidsbank.com)

Merit Badge.com (www.meritbadge.com)

Parent Soup (www.parentsoup.com)

The Smart Guide to Financial Aid (www.finaid.com)

Teach With Movies (www.teachwithmovies.org)

Think Quest (www.thinkquest.com)

Unconventional Ideas (www.unconventionalideas.com)

CHAPTER TEN

Why Every Parent Should Consider Homeschooling

"The thick marble walls of libraries and museums protect our supposed bequest to future ages. How short a vision. Our children are the builders of tomorrow's world—quiet infants, clumsy toddlers, and running, squealing second-graders, whose pliable neurons carry within them all humanity's hope. Their flexible brains have yet to germinate the ideas, the songs, and the societies of tomorrow. They can create the next world or they can annihilate it. In either case, they will do so in our names."

Dr. Thomas Lewis, Dr. Fari Amini, and Dr. Richard Lannon,
A General Theory of Love

WE ALL WANT THE WORLD FOR OUR CHILDREN. We dream about their future from the moment they enter the world. We do what we can as parents to make sure their lives will be rich with opportunities, success, and happiness. Unfortunately, the majority of our nation's school-aged children are unable to look forward to such a future because our public school system is educating them to become citizens in a workplace, economy, and way of life that no longer exists. Although dedicated teachers across the nation give their all to educate over 48 million school-aged children, they can only do so much with antiquated classrooms and inferior teaching methods. Moreover, as Roger Schnak has pointed out in *Coloring Outside the Lines,* the very model of education they are forced to use was developed over a hundred and fifty years ago during the industrial revolution. In today's upwardly mobile, highly literate society, teachers still rely on a system created to produce a factory worker mentality! The students are treated like automobiles in a factory; the teachers are the production line workers moving the automobiles along the assembly line. Students move through classrooms on a factory production line and on a factory production schedule. Teachers administer the same one-size-fits-all education to *every* student—regardless of a child's learning style, intelligence, readiness, interests, or uniqueness. Customized education is not available in our factory schools. Parents are only able to order the same education for their child that every other parent in America does. Daniel Pink discusses the equivalence of the school system and factory life in his book, *Free Agent Nation:* "Compulsory mass schooling . . . equipped generations of future factory workers and middle managers with the basic skills and knowledge they needed on the job . . . Schools had bells; factories had whistles. Schools had report card grades; offices had pay grades."*

While these schools worked in the early Industrial Age, their educational standards are simply inferior and irrelevant in today's economic and social conditions. Clearly, American society has moved way beyond these assembly line principles. Continuing to educate our children to function in an age and economy that no longer exists guarantees their failure. We are the most powerful, creative, and entrepreneurial nation in the world. We can do much better. Accepting and incorporating alternatives to the current school system is not just smart, it's necessary, if our children are to be able to seize all the opportunities that life in America will present to them.

Just as factory schools were created for the business world prevalent in the industrial age, homeschooling and other alternative educational programs are growing to meet the needs of a new business world and a time in our country's history.

*Pink, Daniel, *Free Agent Nation: How America's New Independent Workers are Transforming the Way We Live.* Warner Books: New York, 2001. p. 245.

Daniel Pink talks about the massive change in the American workplace and the types of educational programs that are a by-product of this massive shift in how Americans work.

> Over the past decade, in nearly every industry and region, work has been undergoing perhaps its most significant transformation since Americans left the farm for the factory a century ago. Legions of Americans, and increasingly citizens of other countries as well, are abandoning one of the Industrial Revolution's most enduring legacies—the job—and forging new ways to work. They're becoming self-employed knowledge workers, proprietors of home-based businesses, temps and permatemps, freelancers and e-lancers, independent contractors and independent professionals, micropreneurs and infopreneurs, part-time consultants, interim executives, on-call troubleshooters, and full-time soloists.
>
> . . . Parents and politicians have sensed the need for reform, and have pushed education to the top of the national agenda. Unfortunately, few of the conventional remedies—standardized testing, character training, recertifying teachers—will do much to cure what ails American schools, and may even make things worse. Free agency, though, will force the necessary changes. Look for free agency to accelerate and deepen three incipient movements in education—home schooling, alternatives to traditional high school, and new approaches to adult learning. These changes will prove as path breaking as mass public schooling was a century ago.*

PREPARING INDIVIDUALS

Nearly all of the educators and theorists we've cited in this book have declared the dawning of a renewed age of the individual. Never before have we had so many choices as to where and how we live, when and how we work—in other

*Pink, *Free Agent Nation*, pp. 10–11 and 246–47.

words, the freedom available to us to define our own vision of success. Homeschooling is a method of education that can be customized to honor a child's uniqueness, by helping him discover his special talents and gifts, and is tailored to his readiness and interests. Our current school system can't offer this type of individualized education in a crowded classroom with one teacher and thirty students. Perhaps our current schools will completely reinvent themselves. But will you take a wait-and-see approach when your child's future is at stake?

Although homeschooling is not for everyone, every parent should consider it as a viable option before sending their children off to twelve years of one-size-fits-all, factory education. All parents should first ask themselves a few crucial questions: What will happen to my children's love of learning in these factory schools? Their trust in themselves? Their belief in their uniqueness and special genius? How much of their true potential will survive? Will they survive a model of education that was designed *not* to acknowledge their true potential?

In the age of the individual we now know how to educate the creators of tomorrow's new world—in the ideal classroom, the home. The only question is: *will we?*

As parents we know one thing for sure: the world we want for our children is a world where everyone is valued for their uniqueness, and where each man and woman can make their passion their life's work. Let's teach our children to seize all that our changing world and human potential avails, by creating a superior education for them at home.

The Homeschooling Resource Guide: The Books, Web Sites, Support Groups, and Products You Need

H*OMESCHOOL.COM EMBRACES THE INCREDIBLE diversity of the homeschooling community as well as the diversity of homeschooling resources available. This resource guide has been compiled to help parents make an informed choice in their selection of products and services for their child's home education. Homeschool.com does not necessarily endorse the products and services listed in this guide.*

BOOKS ABOUT HOMESCHOOLING

And What About College?
by Cafi Cohen
Holt/GWS, 2000

Anyone Can Homeschool
by Terry Dorian, Ph.D., and Zan Peters Tyler
Huntington House Publishers, 1996

Basic Steps to Successful Homeschooling
by Vicki Brady
Vital Issues Press, 1996

Beginner's Guide to Homeschooling
by Patrick Farenga
Holt Associates/GWS, 2000

Beyond the American Dream: Lifelong Learning and the Search for Meaning in a Postmodern World
by Charles D. Hayes
Autodidactic Press, 1998

Big Book of Home Learning
by Mary Pride
Home Life, Inc., 1993–2001

Christian Home Educators' Curriculum
by Cathy Duffy
Grove Publishing, 1997

Complete Guide to Homeschooling
by John and Kathy Perry
Lowell House, 2000

The Complete Home Learning Source Book
by Rebecca Rupp
Three Rivers Press, 1998

Deschooling Our Lives
edited by Matt Hern
New Society Publishers, 1996

Dumbing Us Down
by John Taylor Gatto
New Society Publishers, 1991

Family Matters: Why Homeschooling Makes Sense
by David Guterson
A Harvest Book, 1992

The First Year of Homeschooling Your Child
by Linda Dobson
Prima, 2001

Getting a Free Education Without the High Cost of College
by B. R. Christensen
Effective Living Publishing, 1994
1-916-422-8435

Getting Started kit from Homeschool.com
Includes book, videotape, state laws, FAQs, and catalogue
www.Homeschool.com/kit

Home-Based Education: The Informed Choice (Video)
by Brian D. Ray, Ph.D.
NHERI Publications, 1999
1-503-364-1490

Home Educating with Confidence
by Rick and Marilyn Boyer
Holly Hall Publishing, 1996

Homeschoolers' College Admissions Handbook
by Cafi Cohen
Prima, 2000

Homeschooling (audiotape)
by Mary Heinking, M.S.
The Objectivist Center, 1999
1-800-374-1776

Homeschooling Almanac, 2000–2001
by Mary and Michael Leppert
Prima, 1999

Homeschooling America: Getting Started (video)
www.Homeschool.com/video

Homeschooling: A Patchwork of Days
by Nancy Lande
WindyCreek Press, 1996

Homeschooling Book of Answers: The 88 Most Important Questions Answered by Homeschooling's Most Respected Voices
by Linda Dobson
Prima, 1998

The Homeschooling Handbook
by Mary Griffith
Prima, 1999

Homeschooling: The Early Years
by Linda Dobson
Prima, 1999

Homeschooling for Excellence
by David and Micki Colfax
Warner Books, 1988

Home Schooling from Scratch
by Mary Potter Kenyon
Gazelle Publications, 1996
1-800-650-5076

Homeschooling the Middle Years: Homeschooling the 8–12-Year-Old Child
by Shari Henry
Prima, 1999

Homeschooling Odyssey
by Matthew James
Self-Published, 1998
1-503-559-5974

Homeschooling on a Shoestring
by Melissa L. Morgan and Judith Waite Allee
Harold Shaw Publishers, 1999

Home Schooling: The Right Choice!
by Christopher Klicka
Loyal Publishing, 2000

Homeschooling the Teen Years
by Cafi Cohen
Prima, 2000

Homeschool Open House: Interviews with 55 Families
by Nancy Lande
WindyCreek Press, 2000

Homeschool Your Child for Free: More Than 1,200 Smart, Effective, and Practical Resources for Home Education on the Internet and Beyond
by Laura Maery Gold and Joan Zielinski
Prima, 2000

Homeschoolers' Success Stories
by Linda Dobson
Prima, 2000

I Learn Better by Teaching Myself
by Agnes Leistico
Holt Associates, 1997

Learning All the Time
by John Holt
Addison Wesley, 1989

Learning at Home: A Mother's Guide to Homeschooling
by Marty Layne
Sea Change Publications, 1998

Learning Together with Children
by Jeanette Kroese Thomson
Origins Publishing, 1997

Miseducation: Preschoolers at Risk
by David Elkind
Alfred A. Knopf, 1987

Multiple Intelligences: The Theory in Practice
by Howard Gardner
Basic Books, 1993

Real Lives: Eleven Teenagers Who Don't Go to School
by Grace Llewellyn
Lowry House Publishers, 1993

Rebellion with Purpose: A Young Adult's Guide to the Improvement of Self and Society
by Richard V. Sidy
SNS Press, 1993

Strengths of Their Own: Academic Achievement, Family Characteristics, and Longitudinal Traits
by Brian D. Ray, Ph.D.
NHERI Publications, 1997
1-503-364-1490

The Successful Homeschool Family Handbook
by Dr. Raymond and Dorothy Moore
Thomas Nelson Publishers, 1994

Teaching the Trivium: Christian Homeschooling in a Classical Style
by Harvey and Laurie Bluedorn
Trivium Pursuit, 2001

The Teenage Liberation Handbook
by Grace Llewellyn
Lowry House, 1991

The Uncollege Alternative
by Danielle Wood
ReganBooks, 2000

The Unofficial Guide to Homeschooling
by Kathy Ishizuka
IDG Books Worldwide, 2000

The Unschooling Handbook
by Mary Griffith
Prima, 1998

The Well-Trained Mind: A Guide to Classical Education at Home
by Jessie Wise and Susan Wise Bauer
W.W. Norton & Company, 1999

What Your _____ Grader Needs to Know
by E. D. Hirsch, Jr.
Dell Publishing, 1998

HOMESCHOOLING MAGAZINES AND NEWSLETTERS

F.U.N. News (Family Unschoolers Network)
www.unschooling.org
1-888-FUN-7020

Home Education Magazine
www.home-ed-magazine.com
1-800-236-3278

Homefires: The Journal of Homeschooling
www.homefires.com
1-888-4-HOME-ED

Homeschool.com's eZine
www.homeschool.com/subscribe

Homeschooling Today
www.homeschooltoday.com
1-904-475-3088

Options in Learning
www.croton.com/allpie
1-518-392-6900

Practical Homeschooling
www.home-school.com
1-800-346-6322

The Link
www.homeschoolnewslink.com

HOMESCHOOLING WEB SITES

A to Z Home's Cool
www.gomilpitas.com/homeschooling/

Homeschool-Teens-College
www.homeschoolteenscollege.net

Eclectic Homeschool Online
www.eho.org

FamilyEducation.com
www.familyeducation.com

Home Education Magazine
www.home-ed-magazine.com

Homeschool.com
www.Homeschool.com

Homeschool Central
www.homeschoolcentral.com

Home School Legal Defense Association
www.HLSDA.com

Homeschool World
www.home-school.com

The Homeschool Zone
www.homeschoolzone.com

Homeschooling at About.com
www.homeschooling.about.com

Jon's Homeschool Resource Page
www.midnightbeach.com/hs/

National Home Education Network
www.nhen.org

National Home Education Research Institute
www.nheri.org

School Is Dead; Learn in Freedom
www.learninfreedom.org

Unschooling.com
www.unschooling.com

CURRICULUM PROVIDERS

A Beka Books
Christian textbooks, curriculum, and support materials
www.abeka.com/hsc/
1-877-223-5226

Alpha Omega
Provides high-quality Christian homeschool curricula, in a user-friendly format
www.home-schooling.com
1-877-688-2652

Bob Jones University Press
"When home educators went looking for Christian textbooks, we were the first to listen. We are still listening."
www.bjup.com
1-800-845-5731

Calvert School
Calvert School offers a complete fully accredited curriculum for pre-kindergarten through grade eight, delivered right to your door, ready to use with everything you need to teach, from lesson manuals to textbooks and workbooks.
www.calvertschool.org
1-888-487-4652

Christian Liberty Academy
Offers a wide range of textbooks, resources, and services
www.class-homeschools.org/clpress/clpress.htm
1-847-259-4444

Christian Resource Connection
Save 20 to 80 percent on used curriculum and testing materials
1-903-935-0418

Compass Learning, Inc.
Creators of Personal Compass, an interactive multimedia curriculum delivered on CD-ROM that is aligned with national and state standards
www.compasslearning.com
1-800-247-1380

Curriculum Services
Complete, parent-friendly, K–12 program with over eighteen years of experience
www.curriculumservices.com
1-877-702-1419

Destinations
Individually tailored curriculum that uses goal setting to develop confidence and clear direction
http://showcase.netins.net/web/nurture/destinations
1-319-477-3011

Home Study International
Accredited curriculum ranges from preschool through college
www.his.edu
1-800-782-4769

HistorySolutions.com
The first online history workbook that offers interactive simulations
www.homeschool.com/historysolutions

Life in America
World history, American history, English, geography, science, and art, along with large doses of Bible and character
www.LifeinAmerica.com

Robinson Self-Teaching Curriculum
250 books and exams in 22 CD-ROMS ($195)
www.robinsoncurriculum.com
1-248-740-2697

School of Tomorrow
"Parent-friendly" curriculum for grades K–12
www.schooloftomorrow.com
1-800-925-7777

INDEPENDENT STUDY SERVICES

Alger Learning Center
Nationally accredited and specializing in working with students who want to
design their own curriculum
www.independent-learning.com
1-800-595-2630

Desiderata School
An accredited, personalized learning program designed to specifically meet
the individual needs and interests of each student
www.disiderataschool.com

Sylvan Learning Centers
"Sylvan gets results!"
www.educate.com

University of Florida Correspondence Study
Quality Education . . . anytime . . . anywhere
www.correspondencestudy.ufl.edu
1-800-327-4218

PRIVATE DISTANCE-LEARNING SCHOOLS (ELEMENTARY)

Clonlara
All the benefits of home education and the support of private school
www.clonlara.org
1-734-769-4511

Laurel Springs School
Accredited K–12 Distance Learning Program offering exceptional teachers
who provide a flexible curriculum sensitive to each student's individual learning styles
www.laurelsprings.com
1-800-377-5890

PRIVATE DISTANCE-LEARNING SCHOOLS (HIGH SCHOOL)

Citizen's High School
An accredited, independent study high school completion program
www.citizenschool.com
1-800-736-GRAD (4723)

Home Study International
Complete high school program leading to state-approved, regional accredited
diploma
www.his.edu
1-800-782-4769

Indiana University High School
Fully accredited by the North Central Association of Colleges and Schools
http://scs.indiana.edu
1-800-334-1011

Keystone National High School
A leading independent study specialist for over 25 years, Keystone offers more than 35 fully accredited programs for grades 9–12 in all basic subject areas and electives, available in either online or print (correspondence) formats
www.keystonehighschool.com
1-800-255-4937

NorthStar Academy Online
Internet-based and diploma-granting program for students in grades 7–12 from a Christian faith perspective
www.northstar-academy.org
1-888-464-6280

TEST PREPARATION

Perfection Learning
Test preparation for grades 3–12
www.perfectionlearning.com
1-800-762-2999

Regents College
Regents College Examinations are excellent tools for helping homeschooled students demonstrate college level readiness and knowledge
www.regents.edu
1-888-RCEXAMS

TestBuddy.com
"Need more time for the fun stuff?"
www.TestBuddy.com
1-866-311-6500

ART AND MUSIC

How Great Thou Art
A godly perspective on art
www.howgreatthouart.com
1-800-982-DRAW

Meet the Masters
Interactive art education that brings out the creativity in K–8 students
www.meetthemasters.com
1-949-492-1583

Mrs. Music Enterprises
Three great CDs to encourage your child's music appreciation
1-310-472-6875

COLLEGE

Liberty University
"Changing Lives . . . One Degree at a Time"
www.liberty.edu
1-800-543-5317

Mary Baldwin College
Homeschooled young women choose Mary Baldwin College because of "value" and "values"
www.mbc.edu
1-800-468-2262

Regents College
Regents College Examinations are excellent tools for helping homeschooled students demonstrate college level readiness and knowledge
www.regents.edu
1-888-RCEXAMS

University of Florida Correspondence Study
Quality Education . . . anytime . . . anywhere
www.correspondencestudy.ufl.edu
1-800-327-4218

EDUCATIONAL TOYS, KITS, AND GAMES

Creative Teaching Associates
Two hundred quality, nonelectronic, educational games for grade K–12
www.mastercta.com

FatPencil.com
Shopping at FatPencil.com is like shopping at your local educational supply store, except they have more for less
www.FatPencil.com

Hearth Song
Toys you'll feel good about giving
www.hearthsong.com
1-800-533-4397

Alex Toys
Quality creative products that foster personal expression and self-esteem
www.alextoys.com
1-800-666-2539

Back-to-Basics Toys
1-800-356-5360

Chinaberry
A treasure of a catalogue for parents
www.chinaberry.com
1-800-776-2242

Creativity for Kids
Kits bursting with great arts and crafts projects
www.creativityforkids.com
1-800-311-8684 ext 3037

Educational Insights
Where learning is fun!
www.educationalinsights.com
1-800-933-3277

Family Pastimes
Play together not against each other
www.familypastimes.com
1-888-267-4414

Game Wright
Award-winning games that cultivate social interaction
www.gamewright.com
1-617-924-6006

Klutz Press
Fun, how-to books designed for doing, not just reading
www.klutz.com
1-650-857-0888

Learning Curve
Dedicated to encouraging creative and imaginative play
www.learningcurve.com
1-800-704-8697

LEGO Dacta
Educational LEGO kits for school and home
www.lego.com/dacta
1-800-362-4308

Lillian Vernon for Kids
1-800-505-2250

OWI, Inc.
Creative robotic kits
1-800-638-1694

Wild Goose Company
Real Science—Real Fun!
www.wildgoosecompany.com
1-888-621-1040

FOREIGN LANGUAGE COURSES

The Learnables
Easy-to-use self-study language tapes/books available in Spanish, French, German, Russian, Japanese, Chinese, Hebrew, Czech, and English as a foreign language
www.learnables.com
1-800-237-1830

Muzzy, the BBC Language Course for Children
The most complete multimedia program available today to teach your child Spanish, French, German, or Italian
www.early-advantage.com
1-888-248-0480

Power-Glide
The leader in foreign language for home study, classroom, distance learning, and independent study—changing the way the world learns languages!
www.power-glide.com
1-800-596-0910

INTERNET SUPPORT AND SERVICES

HomeSchool Family Network
A dedicated ISP for helping you educate and protect your children while they surf!
www.homeschoolfamilies.net
1-888-811-4785

LANGUAGE ARTS

A Reason for Spelling
Skills for life, values for a lifetime
www.areasonfor.com
1-800-447-4332

A Reason for Writing
Skills for life, values for a lifetime
www.areasonfor.com
1-800-447-4332

Earobics
Software that teaches phonemic awareness, auditory processing, and introductory phonics skills needed to learn to read and spell
www.cogcon.com
1-847-328-8099

ESP Books
Creators of the world-famous Golden Year Books
www.espbooks.com
1-800-643-0280

Frontline Phonics
Start early and give your child the reading edge!

www.frontlinephonics.com
1-800-584-READ

Getty-Dubay
The Italic handwriting series for Kindergarten–6th graders
www.extended.pdx.edu/press
1-800-547-8887 ext. 4891

Hooked On Phonics
A proven system that can help your child become a better, more confident reader in as little as four weeks
www.abcdefg.com
1-800-532-3607

JayMar Services/Archstone Press
Life-changing works and nontraditional published items for improving people's lives
www.jaymarsvcs.com

Let's Go Learn
Homeschool Reading Assessment
www.homeschool.com/reading
1-888-618-READ (U.S. Only)

Perfection Learning
Literature tests, Grammar Works, and Hi-Low Readers for reluctant readers
www.perfectionlearning.com
1-800-831-4190

Progeny Press
Study Guides for a Christian Perspective
Reproducible, comprehensive lessons
www.progenypress.com
1-877-776-4369

Ready Reading
A systematic multisensory beginning reading program found to be successful also with at-risk students
www.readywork.com

Saxon Phonics
Saxon Phonics encourages and provides the skills for children to become life-long readers
www.saxonpub.com
1-800-284-7019

Usborne Books at Home
Usborne Publishing provides affordable educational children's books ideal for teachers, students, homeschoolers, and parents. Every Usborne book is colorful, brilliantly illustrated, and highly interactive.
www.homeschool.com/bookstore/usborne/default.asp
1-800-291-2032

Writing Strands
Writing Strands is the leading, award-winning writing curriculum designed especially for homeschoolers
www.writingstrands.com
1-800-688-5375

MATH

APlusStudent.com
APlusStudent.com is a premier online education company addressing the needs of the K–12 market.
www.APlusStudent.com
1-856-642-9293

Binary Arts
The nation's leading independent manufacturer of brainteaser puzzles, toys, and games
www.binaryarts.com
www.puzzles.com
1-800-468-1864

BoxerMath.com
The Internet's first comprehensive learning environment for math. Grades 3–12. They offer a free two-week trial so you can try before you buy!
www.BoxerMath.com

ETA Cuisenaire
Offers thousands of educational math products that are as effective in home-schools as they are in school classrooms
www.etacuisenaire.com/homeschool.stm
1-800-445-5985

Math Concepts
Imagine strengthening your child's math skills in only 7 to 10 minutes a day and no tedious tests!
www.mathconcepts.com
1-800-574-9936

PCS Edventures
An Internet-delivered educational program designed for families with children ages 6 and up
www.edventures.com
1-800-429-3110

S & S Math Software
Providing software education, development, and consultation since 1979
www.sssoftware.com
1-877-384-3844

Saxon Math
Build your child's confidence in math—use Saxon's mathematics programs for grades K–12
www.saxonpub.com
1-800-284-7019

Scholastix Software
"Let our comprehensive math software propel your child to success in math through explanations, practice, games, and step-by-step graphics that cover all of basic math."
www.homeschool.com/resources/Scholastix/default.asp
1-888-675-7948

ONLINE LEARNING

Alpha Omega Academy On-Line
Offers computer-based education for parents who are wanting to home-school, yet are looking for the teaching and benefits of a private school
www.switched-onschoolhouse.com/aoao
1-877-688-2652

Aunt Ellen Learning Systems
Fun, interactive computer skills training for children
www.auntellen.com
1-800-996-2791

ChildU
Interactive K–7 curriculum available directly through Homeschool.com!
www.homeschool.com/childu/
1-877-4ChildU

Expressways to Learning
Multisensory learning systems designed to remediate reading comprehension

and math, using a computer-based multimedia format. Specializing in helping children with special needs.
www.expresswaystolearning.com

K12.com
Education for a lifetime
www.k12.com

SCIENCE

American Science & Surplus
Offers science kits, educational toys, school supplies, arts and crafts items, hobby tools, scales, lab gloves, housewares, electronics, and much more—all at discount closeout prices
www.sciplus.com
1-847-982-0870

Carolina Biological
Science products for school and home
www.carolina.com
1-800-334-5551

Delta Education
Some of the most creative and colorful hands-on learning products to help your children explore the world of math and science
www.delta-ed.com
1-800-442-5444

Edventures.com
An Internet-delivered educational program designed for families with children ages 6 and up
www.edventures.com
1-800-429-3110

Environmental Media
An environmental education company that produces and distributes quality media to support environmental education
www.envmedia.com
1-800-368-3382

Hands-On Science
Science kits for elementary and middle-school children
www.science-enrichment.com
1-918-664-4561

Interactive Learning, Inc.
Interactive software for biology, chemistry, and physics
www.highergrades.com
1-877-GRADES 1

The Jason Project
For over ten years, the Jason Project has put adventure and thrill of discovery into science education
www.jason.org
1-888-527-6600

Science Kit & Boreal Laboratories
Award-winning microscopes and more!
www.sciencekit.com
1-800-828-7777

Southern Scientific
One-stop science store for all courses and levels of science
www.southernscientific.com
1-800-748-8735

Ring of Fire
Fun and inexpensive geology kits

www.sciencekitsforkids.com
1-888-785-5439

SOCIAL STUDIES

Bluestocking Press
Publisher of the Uncle Eric books and a supplier of "original source" materials and other history products
www.bluestockingpress.com
1-800-959-8586

StoriesPast.com
You will be transported back into the past with this exciting new interactive online program
www.storiespast.com

World Newsmap of the Month
The only comprehensive poster curriculum that combines current events with geography
1-847-831-4020

SOFTWARE AND VIDEOS

Classroom Visuals.com
Complete educational video membership service
www.classroomvisuals.com
1-888-560-4787

Inspired Idea
Innovative Christ-centered learning materials including software, multimedia curriculum, and special needs
www.InspiredIdea.com
1-480-940-6147

Muzzy, the BBC Language Course for Children
The most complete multimedia program available today to teach your child Spanish, French, German, or Italian
www.early-advantage.com
1-888-248-0480

Wildridge Software
Popular multimedia programs called "Math & Music" and "Stars & Stories"
www.wildridge.com
1-888-244-4379

SPECIAL NEEDS & GIFTED RESOURCES

The Dyslexia Reader Newsletter
1-888-999-3324

Expressways to Learning
Multisensory learning systems designed to remediate reading comprehension and math, using a computer-based multimedia format specializing in helping children with special needs
www.expresswaystolearning.com

The Gift of Dyslexia: Why Some of the Smartest People Can't Read and How They Can Learn by Ronald Davis, et al.

Prufrock Press
The leading publisher for gifted education
www.prufrock.com
1-800-998-2208

Homeschooling Support Groups

ALABAMA

BRAINS (Baldwin Regional Association of Independent Nontraditional
  Schools)
BRAINS@firehousemail.com
P.O. Box 1765
Bay Minette, AL 36507-1765

Central Alabama Resource for home educators (CARE)
Mi4Angels@aol.com

Christian Home Education Fellowship of Alabama (CHEF)
Pres@ALHOME.com
P.O. Box 20208
Montgomery, AL 36120-0208
1-334-288-7229

Alabama Home Educators Network
KaeKaeB@aol.com
605 Mountain Gap Dr.
Huntsville, AL 35803
1-205-882-0208

Alabama Independent Church School Association—The Alabama Homeschooling Organization
P.O. Box 5273
Glencoe, AL 35905-0273
1-256-492-1668

Southwest Alabama Home Educators
angels@in-city.com
6408 Middle Ring Court
Mobile, AL 36608
1-334-443-7243

HEART
mirator@educationalfreedom.com
P.O. Box 1159
Tallevast, AL 34270

ALASKA

Homeschoolers Unlimited
Sue@homeschoolersunlimited.com
7390 J Street #B
Elmendorf AFB, AK 99506

Alaska Homeschool Network
AHN@akhomeschool.net
P.O. Box 3142
Palmer, AK 99645

Alaska Private and Home Educators Association (APHEA)
networknews@gci.net
P.O. Box 141764
Anchorage, AK 99514
1-907-566-3450

Christian Home Educators of Kodiak
chek@unforgettable.com
12174 Gara Dr.
Kodiak, AK 99615
1-907-487-2471

ARIZONA

Apache Junction Unschoolers
ajunschl@aol.com
P.O. Box 2880
Apache Junction, AZ 85217

Scottsdale Unschoolers
maofdb@aol.com

Sonoran Desert Homeschoolers
hozho@homestead.com
3450 S. Jamie Ave.
Tucson, AZ 85735
1-520-883-1543

Arizona Families for Home Education
AFHE@Primenet.com
P.O. Box 4461
Scottsdale, AZ 85261-4461
1-800-929-3927

The Salt Seller
SaltSeller@aol.com
P.O. Box 56701
Phoenix, AZ 85079-6701
1-602-249-2699

Valley Secular Homeschooling
laf85220@yahoo.com
416 N. 104th St.
Apache Junction, AZ 85220
1-480-837-1939

West Side Home Educators
cmmahar@apsc.com
8622 W. Purdue Ave.
Peoria, AZ 85345

Phoenix Learning Alternatives Network
curtkar@home.com
8835 N. 47th Place
Phoenix, AZ 85028
1-602-483-3381

ARKANSAS

Home Educators of Arkansas (HEAR) Coalition of Arkansas Parents (CAP)
Heareport@juno.com
P.O. Box 192455
Little Rock, AR 72219
1-501-847-4942

Arkansas Christian Home Education Association (ACHEA)
P.O. Box 4025
North Little Rock, AR 72190
1-501-758-9099

The Education Alliance
edu@familycouncil.org
414 S. Pulaski St., Suite 2

Little Rock, AR 72201-2930
1-501-375-7000

CALIFORNIA

Bay Area Homelearners
hawk141@earthlink.net
Sunnyvale, CA

Fresno Homeschoolers
quest_j@pacbell.net
P.O. Box 4098
Fresno, CA 93744

HomeSchool Association of California
info@hsc.org
P.O. Box 868
Davis, CA 95617
1-888-472-4440

Inclusive Homeschoolers of Carmel Valley/Monterey
kirbyfamily@earthlink.net
Carmel Valley, CA
1-831-372-4996

M.U.G.S. Mothers of Upper Grade Students
point5pub@msn.com
P.O. Box 1032
Visalia, CA 93279-0132

Bay Hills Home Educators Support Group
DcnAileen@home.com
1529 Lafayette

Alameda, CA 94541
1-510-351-5449

Bayshore Homeschoolers
BayShorEdu@aol.com
P.O. Box 13038
Long Beach, CA 90803
1-562-434-3940

Sonoma County California Home Schooling Group
jcarter3@hotmail.com
Sonoma, CA

Christian Home Educators Association of California
P.O. Box 2009
Norwalk, CA 90651-2009
1-800-564-2432

Valley Home Educators
VHELEISA@aol.com
P.O. Box 4016
Modesto, CA 95352-4016
1-209-527-5471

Yolo County Homeschoolers
shonkfamily@juno.com
1301 Arena Drive
Davis, CA 95616
1-530-759-1106

Homeschool Support Network
livinglighthouse@yahoo.com
Paradise, CA
1-530-872-2975

High Desert Homeschoolers
taylors@mscomm.com
Victorville/Apple Valley/Hesperia, CA
1-760-956-1588

Redding Homeschool Network
erinf@c-zone.net
2205 Hilltop Dr.
Redding, CA 96002
1-530-347-5249

World Class Seekers–Southern California's Alternative Homeschool Group
WorldClassSeeker@aol.com
P.O. Box 1283
Whittier, CA 90609

Venture Home Schoolers Resources
ventureschool@hotmail.com
231 Market P1#328
San Ramon, CA 94583

Twin Ridges Homeschool Support Group
cinpaw@juno.com
Grass Valley, CA
1-530-274-8646

South Bay Homeschool Network
mav1@earthlink.net
P.O. Box 921
Manhattan Beach, CA 90267-0921

California Homeschool Network
mail@cahomeschoolnet.org
P.O. Box 55485

Hayward, CA 94545
1-800-327-5339

COLORADO

Christian Home Educators of Colorado
office@chec.org
10431 South Parker Road
Parker, CO 80134
1-720-842-4852

Columbine Homeschool Connection
unschoolmom2@yahoo.com
Littleton, CO
1-303-948-3308 or 933-6719

Denver Northwest Homeschool Community
cthughes@home.com
3540 Vrain Street
Denver, CO 80212
1-203-234-1304

Independent Network of Creative Homeschoolers
1499 S. Lima Street
Aurora, CO 80012
1-303-751-6421

Colorado Home Educators' Association
pinewood@dash.com
3043 South Laredo Circle
Aurora, CO 80013
1-303-441-9938

Colorado Springs Homeschool Support Group
board@hschool.com
P.O. Box 26117
Colorado Springs, CO 80936
1-719-598-2636

Secular Homeschool Support Group
shssg@mindspring.com
2407 Marlborough Place
Colorado Springs, CO 80909
1-719-634-4098

West River Unschoolers
wracademy@aol.com
779 Jasmine Ct.
Grand Junction, CO 81506
1-970-241-4137

CONNECTICUT

Connecticut Home Educators Association
nedvare@ntplx.net
22 Wildrose Ave.
Guilford, CT 06437
1-860-233-1111

Connecticut Home Educators Association
Becherhomeschool@aol.com
P.O. Box 242
New Hartford, CT 06057
1-203-781-8569

Connecticut Homeschool Network
CtHmschlNtwk@aol.com
47 Daniel St.
East Hampton, CT 06424
1-860-267-5305

Home Educators of the Northwest Hills
cynthia.huntoon@snet.net
22 Chatham Ct.
Goshen, CT 06756
1-860-491-5305

Mountain Laurel Homeschool Support Group
MZKZNZJZ@aol.com
783 Ward Lane
Cheshire, CT 06410
1-203-271-0575

The Education Association of Christian Homeschoolers (TEACH)
teachinfo@pobox.com
282 Camp St.
Plainville, CT 06062
1-800-205-8744

DELAWARE

Brandywine Valley Home Education Resource Organization
bvheroes@hotmail.com
P.O. Box 117
Claymont, DE 19803
1-302-478-4430

Delaware Home Education Association
P.O. Box 1003
Dover, DE 19903
1-302-429-0515

Support for Home Educators and Resources in Dover
tdand4lk@yahoo.com
4161 Arthursville Road
Hartly, DE 19953
1-302-492-0869

FLORIDA

Big Bend Unschooling Group
shelah2@myTalk.com
19243 North by NW Road
Tallahassee, FL 32310
1-850-576-1551

Broward County Parent Support Group
info@browardcountypsg.org
7780 N.W. 39th Street
Hollywood, FL 33024
1-954-938-5442

Christian Home Educators of Florida
chef@christianhomeeducatorsofflorida.com
P.O. Box 5393
Clearwater, FL 33758-5393

Florida Parent Educators Association
office@fpea.com
P.O. Box 850685

Jacksonville Beach, FL 32240
1-877-275-3732

Home Educators Assistance League
3343 Shoal Creek Cove
Crestview, FL 32539
1-904-682-2422

Home Educators Lending Parents Support
Krista@HelpsOnline.org
5941 NW 14 Court
Ft. Lauderdale, FL 33313
1-954-791-9733

Homeschool Alternatives of Pinellas County
homeschoolalt@aol.com
7037 32nd Avenue North
St. Petersburg, FL 33710-1406
1-727-381-4259

South County Home Schoolers
info@southcountyhomeschoolers.org
Delray Beach, FL
1-561-638-2602

South Florida Homeschool Association
AmyKCA@aol.com
P.O. Box 840554
Pembroke Pines, FL 33084
1-954-435-9867

HEAT/Teaching Our Own
teachingourown@earthlink.net
155 Flamingo Drive

Boynton Beach, FL 33435
1-561-493-3679

Home Educated Activities Teams, Inc.
PinellasHEAT@aol.com
5688 18th Ave. S.
Gulfport, FL 33707
1-727-347-8259

Home Education and Resources and Information, Inc. (HERI)
herijax@yahoo.com
7572 Wheat Road
Jacksonville, FL 32224
1-904-783-8197

West Florida Home Education Support League
2boys@pcola.gulf.net
P.O. Box 11720
Pensacola, FL 32524
1-850-995-9444

GEORGIA

Atlanta Alternative Education Network
1158 McConnell Dr.
Atlanta, GA 30033
1-404-636-6348

Coweta Home Educators' Association
chea@charter-nn.com
9 Ashley Oaks Lane
Newnan, GA 30263
1-770-502-9375

Georgia Home Education Association
ghea@mindspring.com
245 Buckeye Lane
Fayetteville, GA 30214
1-770-461-3657

L.L.G.-Lifetime Learners of Georgia
mrslarak@yahoo.com
861 Franklin Road, Bldg. 2., Apt. 14
Marietta, GA 30067
1-770-419-8680

Home Education Information Resource (H.E.I.R.)
info@heir.org
P.O. Box 2111
Roswell, GA 30077-2111
1-404-681-4347

Augusta Area Home Education Network
augustahen@yahoo.com
P.O. Box 15963
Augusta, GA 30919-1963
1-706-868-5666

Thomasville Regional Home School Co-op
mhanna@rose.net
P.O. Box 326
Barwick, GA 31720
1-912-735-4356

Valdosta Area Homeschooling Association
vahaga@geocities.com
116 Starmount Drive

Valdosta, GA 31605
1-912-249-0809

Parent Educators Association for Children at Home
peachhomeschool@juno.com
P.O. Box 1743
Buford, GA 24482
1-770-969-5872

HAWAII

Hawaii Homeschool Association
HawaiiHomeschoolers@hotmail.com
P.O. Box 893513
Mililani, HI 96789
1-808-944-3339

Homeschool Adventure: Program for Parents and Youngsters
777 Kolani Place
Wailuku, HI 96793
1-808-242-8225

Kauai Home Educators Association
Jeanne Ferrari Amas
swimmerjean98@yahoo.com
1-808-245-7867

IDAHO

Advocates for Home Education
AdvoHomeEd@aol.com
P.O. Box 2742

Pocatello, ID 83206
1-208-234-7876

Idaho Home Educators
P.O. Box 1324
Meridian, ID 83680
1-208-323-0230

Idaho Intermountain Regional Homeschoolers
we-teach@srv.net
204 5th Street
Idaho Falls, ID 83401
1-208-522-1536

NACHAN (National Challenged Homeschoolers Associated Network)
nachanews@aol.com
P.O. Box 39
Porthill, ID 83583
1-208-267-6246

Family Unschooling Network
ndjensen@quest.net
1809 North 7th Street
Boise, ID 83702
1-208-345-2703

ILLINOIS

Home Oriented Unique Schooling Experience (HOUSE)
illinois_house@hotmail.com
2508 East 22nd Place
Sauk Village, IL 60411
1-708-758-7374

Illinois Christian Home Educators
info@iche.org
P.O. Box 775
Harvard, IL 60033
1-815-943-7882

Islamic Homeschooling Education Network
ILYASAH@aol.com
241 Meadowbrook Drive
Bolingbrook, IL 60440-2435

Jewish Homeschool Association of Greater Chicago
BHP@BnosHenya.org
1-773-764-5137

Northside Unschoolers Group
wini@winifredhaun.org
4225 N. Oakley Ave.
Chicago, IL 60618-2909
1-773-478-6938

INDIANA

Families Learning Together
whemul@earthlink.net
1714 East 51st Street
Indianapolis, IN 46205
1-317-255-9298

HomeSchools United, Inc.
vtalex@indy.net
P.O. Box 4002
Anderson, IN 46012
1-765-683-2421

Indiana Association of Home Educators
850 North Madison
Greenwood, IN 46142
1-317-859-1202

Indianpolis Unschoolers
IndianapolisUnschoolers@msn.com
7940 E. SR 334
Zionsville, IN 46077
1-317-873-1185

Life Education and Resource Network
nancyw@bluemarble.net
9998 West State Road
Bloomington, IN 47404

Roman Catholic Home Educators of Indiana (RCHEI)
info@fchei.org
P.O. Box 858
Fishers, IN 46038
1-317-767-5217

IOWA

Iowans Dedicated to Educational Alternatives
hisinfo@juno.com
3296 Linn-Buchanan Rd.
Sioux City, IA 51106
1-319-224-3675

Network of Iowa Christian Home Educators
niche@netins.net
P.O. Box 158

Dexter, IA 50070
1-515-830-1614

KANSAS

Christian Home Educators Confederation of Kansas
info@kansashomeschool.org
P.O. Box 3968
Wichita, KS 67201
1-316-945-0810

Circle of Homeschoolers and Unschoolers in Central Kansas Learning
    Eclectically
RR1 Box 28A
Rush Center, KS 67575
1-913-372-4457

Heartland Area Homeschoolers' Association
823 West Street
Emporia, KS 66801
1-316-343-3696

Lawrence Area Unaffiliated Group of Homeschoolers
RR 1 Box 496
Perry, KS 66073
1-913-597-5579

KENTUCKY

Barren River Home School Association
laffinatu2@hotmail.com
130 Freestone Court

Bowling Green, KY 42103
1-270-782-7384

Bluegrass Home Educators
bhe@ky-on-line.com
600 Shake Rag Road
Waynesburg, KY 40489

Christian Home Educators of Kentucky
chek@kvnet.org
691 Howardstown Road
Hodgensville, KY 42748
1-270-358-9270

Kentucky Home Education Association
katy@mis.net
P.O. Box 81
Winchester, KY 40392-0081
1-859-737-3338

Morehead Area Home Educators
moonwind@zoomnet.net
80 Kimberly Lane
Clearfield, KY 40313
1-606-784-4231

LOUISIANA

Homeschoolers Learning from Mother Earth
14189 Ridge Road
Prairieville, LA 70769

Louisiana Home Education Network
webmaster@la-home-education.com
602 W. Prien Lake Road
Lake Charles, LA 70601

Wild Azalea Unschoolers
wildazaleas@hotmail.com
6055 General Meyer Avenue
New Orleans, LA 70131
1-504-392-5647

Westbank Homeschool Organization (WHO)
whoedu@bellsouth.net
569 Marrero Rd.
Westwego, LA 70073

Christian Home Education Fellowship of Louisiana
chefofla@hotmail.com
P.O. Box 74292
Baton Rouge, LA 70874-4292
1-888-876-2433

MAINE

Central Maine Self-Learners
cmslhomeschool@aol.com
36 Country Acres
Monmouth, ME 04259
1-207-933-5055

Homeschool Associates
info@homeschoolassociates.com
25 Willow St.

Lewiston, ME 04240
1-207-777-1700

Homeschool Support Network
hsn@homeeducator.com
P.O. Box 708
Gray, ME 04039
1-207-657-6889

Maine Home Education Association
P.O. Box 421
Popsham, ME 04086
1-800-520-0577

Homeschoolers of Maine
homeschool@midcoast.com
337 Hatchet Mountain Road
Hope, ME 04847
1-207-763-4251

Homeschoolers of Northern Maine
jetkat@bangornews.infi.net
337 Hatchet Mountain Road
Hope, ME 04847
1-207-476-8904

MARYLAND

Christian Home Educators Network
chenmaster@chenmd.org
P.O. Box 2010
Ellicott City, MD 21043
1-301-474-9055

Columbia Homeschool Community
sunnyspring@excite.com
6272 Sunny Spring
Columbia, MD 21044-3737
1-301-596-8052

Eastern Shore Home School Association
scribblers2@earthlink.net
31905 Sutherland Drive
Salisbury, MD 21804

Glen Burnie Homeschool Support Group
HS6Whetzel@aol.com
6514 Dolphin Court
Glen Burnie, MD 21061

Homesteaders Home School Support Group
gdmyers@erols.com
10001 Route 108
Columbia, MD 21044

Maryland Home Education Association
9085 Flamepool Way
Columbia, MD 21045
1-410-730-0073

North County Home Educators
NCHE@IQCweb.com
1688 Belhaven Woods Court
Pasadena, MD 21122-3727
1-410-437-5109

Walkersville Christian Family Schools (WCFS)
info@wcfs.edu

4 West Main St.
Thurmont, MD 21788-1824
1-301-271-0123

MASSACHUSETTS

Co-op Homeschool Support Group
coophsg@gis.net
90 Keyes Road
Gardner, MA 01440
1-978-632-9089

Homeschooling Together
ses@world.std.com
24 Avon Place
Arlington, MA 02474-6618

Shadows on the Shore–Cape Cod Homeschooling Network
P.O. Box 533
Harwich, MA 02645
1-508-430-7122

Massachusetts Home Learning Association
lisawood@aol.com
P.O. Box 1558
Marstons Mills, MA 02648
1-508-249-9056

Massachusetts Homeschool Organization of Parent Educators (Mass HOPE)
info@masshope.org
5 Atwood Road
Cherry Valley, MA 01611-3332
1-508-755-4467

The Family Resource Center
BigBear001@aol.com
19 Cedarview Street
Salem, MA 01970
1-978-741-7449

South Shore Homeschoolers
87 Snell Avenue
Brockton, MA 02402
1-508-697-9124

Pathfinder Learning Center
plc@valinet.com
256 North Pleasant Street
Amherst, MA 01002
1-413-253-9412

Cape Ann Homeschoolers
grshank@gis.net
6 Davis Street
Gloucester, MA 01930-3839
1-978-281-6927

MICHIGAN

Christian Home Educators of Michigan
P.O. Box 2357
Farmington Hills, MI 48333
1-248-380-3611

Hillsdale Area Homeschoolers
klinefam@dmci.net
5151 Barker Road

Jonesville, MI 49250
1-517-287-5565

Kalamazoo Area Homeschool Association
P.O. Box 2214
Portage, MI 49081-2214
1-616-324-1924

REACH—Restoring Education and Cherishing Home
abmorris@home.com
2525 Patrick Henry St.
Auburn Hills, MI 48326
1-248-377-1513

Hillsdale Area Homeschoolers
klinefam@dmci.net
5151 Barker Road
Jonesville, MI 49250
1-517-287-5565

Families Active in Studies and Teaching
emmanuel@tir.com
4061 Holt Road
Holt, MI 48842-1843
1-517-699-2728

Families Learning and Schooling at Home (FLASH)
21671 B Drive North
Marshall, MI 49068
1-616-781-1069

MINNESOTA

Creative Twin Cities Homeschoolers
creativehomeschoolers@yahoo.com
1439 Hayes Road
Apple Valley, MN 55124

Cultural Home Educators Association (CHEA)
bgabbs@yahoo.com
2324 University Avenue
St. Paul, MN 55005

Minnesota Association of Christian Home Educators
MACHE@ISD.NET
P.O. Box 32308
Fridley, MN 55432-0308
1-612-717-9070

Minnesota Homeschoolers Alliance
mha@homeschoolers.org
P.O. Box 23072
Richfield, MN 55423
1-612-288-9662

Home Educators and Youth (HEY)
homeeducatorsandyouth@yahoo.com
7111 Giants Ridge Road
Embarrass, MN 55732
1-218-984-3503

MISSISSIPPI

Home Educators of Central Mississippi
HECM@webmail.bellsouth.net

102 Hollow Hill Dr.
Florence, MS 39073
1-601-978-2204

Mississippi Home Educators Association
109 Reagan Ranch Road
Laurel, MS 39440
1-601-649-6432

Oxford Homeschool Network
shughart@watervalley.net
21 County Road 3024
Oxford, MS 38655

MISSOURI

Let Education Always Remain Natural (LEARN)
Kwilson898@kclearn.org
P.O. Box 10105
Kansas City, MO 64171
1-913-383-7888

Missouri Association of Teaching Christian Homes
match@match-inc.org
2203 Rhonda Drive
West Plains, MO 65775-1615
1-417-255-2824

St. Louis Homeschool Network
regtill@swbell.net
3862 Flora Place
St. Louis, MO 63110
1-314-664-5566

St. Louis Secular Homeschoolers Co-op
unschool@swbell.net
6628 Wise Ave.
St. Louis, MO 63139
1-636-441-0708

MONTANA

Bozeman Homeschool Network
dalton@ycsi.net
8799 Huffman Lane
Bozeman, MT 59715
1-406-586-3499

Montana Coalition of Home Educators
P.O. Box 43
Gallatin Gateway, MT 59730
1-406-587-6163

MontanaHomeschoolers@egroups.com
hsmick@aol.com
719A Gumwood Street
Great Falls, MT 59405
1-406-453-5592

NEBRASKA

Gardener Home School Support Group
rachellewhaley@hotmail.com

LEARN
7741 East Avon Lane

Lincoln, NE 68505-2043
1-402-488-7741

Nebraska Christian Home Educators Association
nchea@alltel.net
P.O. Box 57041
Lincoln, NE 68505-7041
1-402-423-4297

NEVADA

Home Schools United—Vegas Valley
homeschooluvv@yahoo.com
P.O. Box 93564
Las Vegas, NV 89193
1-702-870-9566

Homeschool Melting Pot
homeschoolmeltingpot@yahoo.com
1178 Antelope Valley Ave.
Henderson, NV 89012
1-702-269-9101

Northern Nevada Home Schools, Inc.
NHHS@aol.com
P.O. Box 21323
Reno, NV 89515
1-702-852-6647

The Association of Home Schooling Families
SonCityMinistries@juno.com
1433 N. Jones Ave.
Las Vegas, NV 89108
1-702-457-1509

NEW HAMPSHIRE

Lebanon Homeschooling Support Group
karen-L-B@excite.com
RR2 Rudsburo Rd. #37
Enfield, NH 03748
1-603-448-5929

New Hampshire Homeschooling Resources
mwatts@dimentech.com
530 Newmarket Road
Warner, NH 03278
1-603-456-2041

New Hampshire Alliance for Home Education
17 Preserve Dr.
Nashua, NH 03060
1-603-880-8629

New Hampshire Homeschooling Coalition
webmaster@nhhomeschooling.org
P.O. Box 2224
Concord, NH 03304-2224
1-603-539-7233

NEW JERSEY

Education Network of Christian Home Schoolers of New Jersey
120 Mayfair Lane
Mt. Laurel, NJ 08054
1-609-222-4283

Homeschoolers of Central New Jersey
kfridkis@kldigital.com
116 Mountain View Road
Princeton, NJ 08540
1-609-333-1119

Homeschoolers of South New Jersey
Tutor@Pulsar.net
1239 Whitaker Avenue
Millville, NJ 08332
1-609-327-1224

New Jersey Homeschool Association
njha@geocities.com
P.O. Box 1386
Medford, NJ 08055
1-609-670-1838

Unschooling Families Support Group of Central New Jersey
150 Folwell Station Road
Jobstown, NJ 08041
1-609-723-1524

NEW MEXICO

Christian Association of Parent Educators
cape-nm@juno.com
P.O. Box 25046
Albuquerque, NM 87125
1-505-898-8548

Homeschooling PACT—Parents and Children Together
Homeschooling-PACT@rocketmail.com

P.O. Box 961
Portales, NM 88130
1-505-359-1618

New Mexico Family Educators
P.O. Box 92276
Albuquerque, NM 87199-2276
1-505-275-7053

New Mexico Homeschooling
SandraDodd@aol.com
2905 Tahiti Ct. NE
Albuquerque, NM 87112
1-505-299-2476

New Mexico Tumbleweeds
monimiura@yahoo.com
5909 Buena Vista NW
Albuquerque, NM 87114
1-505-899-6916

NEW YORK

APPLE Family and Homeschool Group
applefamilygroup@yahoo.com
P.O. Box 2036
North Babylon, NY 11703
1-631-243-5821

Buffalo Area Homeschooling Association
Stannehill@aol.com
8750 Tonawanda Creek Road
Clarence Center, NY 12477
1-716-741-4755

Loving Education at Home (LEAH)
info@leah.org
P.O. Box 438
Fayetteville, NY 13066-0438
1-518-756-9773

Families for Home Education
3219 Coulter Road
Cazenovia, NY 13035
1-315-655-2574

Alliance for Parental Involvement in Education
allpie@taconic.net
P.O. Box 59
East Chatham, NY 12060-0059
1-518-392-6900

Alternative Education Resource Organization
jerryaero@aol.com
417 Roslyn Road
Roslyn Heights, NY 11577
1-800-769-4171

Syracuse-area Homeschooler's Association (SaHA)
beiji99@yahoo.com
201 Milnor Ave.
Syracuse, NY 13224
1-315-446-3068

Tri-County Homeschoolers
chofer@croton.com
P.O. Box 48
Ossining, NY 14850
1-914-941-5607

New York City Home Educators Alliance (NYCHEA)
8 East 2nd Street
New York, NY 10003
1-212-505-9884

New York Home Educators Network
mary_okeeffee@post.harvard.edu
2255 Algonquin Road
Niskayuna, NY 12309
1-518-584-9110

New York State Home Education News
ALLPIESR@aol.com
P.O. Box 59
East Chatham, NY 12060
1-518-392-6900

Woodstock Home Educators Network (WHEN)
msklaroff@ulster.net
12 Cantine's Island
Saugerties, NY 12477

NORTH CAROLINA

Families Learning Together
cn2464@coastalnet.com
1670 NC 33 W
Chocowinity, NC 27817

Native Americans for Home Education (NAHE)
Nuwahti@yahoo.com
P.O. Box 464
Bostic, NC 28018

Zebulon Area Home Educators
gcstilley@aol.com
888 Carlyle Road
Zebulon, NC 27597
1-919-404-0898

Cary Homeschoolers
bookwoman@rosen.com
114 W. Camden Forest Dr.
Cary, NC 27511
1-919-851-5157

Relaxed Homeschoolers
browningdk@netzero.net
8295 Scarlet Oak Court
Harrisburg, NC 28075
1-704-454-5780

North Carolinians for Home Education
nche@mindspring.com
419 North Boylan Avenue
Raleigh, NC 27603-1211
1-919-834-6243

NORTH DAKOTA

North Dakota Home School Association
ndhsa@wdata.com
P.O. Box 7400
Bismarck, ND 58507
1-701-223-4080

OHIO

Families Unschooling in the Neighborhood—Mid-Ohio
laurie@redbird.net
5668 Township Road
Mount Gilead, OH 43338
1-419-947-6351

Home Education Resource Center of Central Ohio
chirsoco@aol.com
3589 East Main Street
Columbus, OH 43227
1-614-237-0004

Learning in Family Environments
Lifehmsl@aol.com
P.O. Box 2512
Columbus, OH 43216
1-614-241-6957

Our (Ohio's) Uniquely Challenged Homeschoolers (OUCH)
RCHOSEN@juno.com
30213 Robert Street
Wickliffe, OH 44092
1-444-944-4782 (mailbox44)

Association of Ohio Homeschoolers
3636 Paris Boulevard
Westerville, OH 43081

Ohio Home Educator's Network
ohen@grafixbynix.com
P.O. Box 38132
Olmsted Falls, OH 44138

Home Oriented Parents Educators of NE Ohio
Kwbcm@sssnet.com
P.O. Box 1482
Akron, OH 44309-1482

Newark Area Home Learners
lepperk@infinet.com
3790 Milner Road
Newark, OH 43055
1-740-366-3802

OKLAHOMA

Cornerstone for the Tulsa Area
ckw4162@juno.com
P.O. Box 459
Tulsa, OK 74073-0459
1-918-250-4953

Eclectic Home Educators
cherriewebb@juno.com
5200 N. Peneil # 38
Bethany, OK 73008
1-405-787-8893

Home Educators Resource Organization (HERO) of Oklahoma
HERO@OklahomaHomeschooling.org
302 North Coolidge
Enid, OK 73703
1-580-446-5679

Oklahoma Home Educators' Network
Teresa Robinson

OKHEdNet@aol.com
P.O. Box 1420
Blanchard, OK 73010
1-405-980-3863

Tulsa Home Educators Coalition
P.O. Box 813
Glenpool, OK 74033
1-918-322-3984

OREGON

Greater Portland Homeschoolers
gphnews@hotmail.com
P.O. Box 82415
Portland, OR 97282
1-503-241-5350

Homeschooler's Educational Resources of Oregon
emailherogroup@aol.com
1478 Morrow Road
Medford, OR 97504
1-541-840-0549

Jewish Home Educators Network of Portland, Oregon
melcro@coho.net

Oregon Christian Home Education Association Network
oceanet@oceanetwork.org
2515 NEN 37th Ave.
Portland, OR 97212
1-503-288-1285

Oregon Home Education Network (OHEN)
ohen@teleport.com
P.O. Box 218
Beaverton, OR 97075-0218
1-503-321-5166

PENNSYLVANIA

Central Philadelphia Homeschoolers
vallone@drexel.edu
216 South Bonsall Street
Philadelphia, PA 19103
1-215-592-7510

Erie Area Homeschoolers
CBDay1220@msn.com
1229 Villa Sites Road
Harborcreek, PA 16421
1-814-899-7010

Homeschoolers Association of Warren County
Cyndi@Penn.com
RR 1, Box 87B1
Youngsville, PA 16371
1-814-489-3366

Pennsylvania Home Education Network (PHEN)
285 Allegheny Street
Meadville, PA 16335
1-412-561-5288

Pennsylvania Home Education News
Karenleven@aol.com

P.O. Box 305
Summerhill, PA 15958
1-814-495-5651

Pennsylvania Homeschoolers Association
richmans@pahomeschoolers.com
RR 2, Box 117
Kittanning, PA 16201

The Natural Learners
dbyrnes@bellatlantic.net
610 Speedwell Forge Road
Lititz, PA 17543
1-717-394-2024

York Home School Association
YHSA@juno.com
981 E. Canal Road
Dover, PA 17315-2717
1-717-292-5379

RHODE ISLAND

Rhode Island Guild of Home Teachers (RIGHT)
right_right@mailexcite.com
P.O. Box 11
Hope, RI 02831
1-401-821-7700

SOUTH CAROLINA

Home Organization of Parent Educators
epeeler@awod.com

1697 Dotterer's Run
Charleston, SC 29414
1-803-763-7833

I.N.C.H. Inclusive Network of Columbia Homeschoolers
INCH@teacher.com
243 Southlake Rd.
Columbia, SC 29223
1-803-788-7110

N.I.C.H.E. Network of Inclusive Coastal Home Educators
photo6keiki@sc.rr.com
113 Twin Oak Court
Myrtle Beach, SC 29572
1-843-449-4902

South Carolina Homeschool Alliance
ConnectSC@aol.com
1679 Memorial Park Road, Suite 179
Lancaster, SC 29720

Tri-County Educational Association of Community Homeschoolers
teachhomeschool@yahoo.com
P.O. Box 651
Summerville, SC 29484

SOUTH DAKOTA

Homeschooling Network of South Dakota
rsc218@aol.com
P.O. Box 1017
Rapid City, SD 57700-1017
1-605-393-2385 or 388-9385

South Dakota Home School Association
P.O. Box 882
Sioux Falls, SD 57101-0882
1-605-338-9689

Western Dakota Christian Home Schools
P.O. Box 528
Black Hawk, SD 55718
1-605-923-1893

TENNESSEE

Memphis Home Education Association
MHEA@MemphisHomeEd.org
P.O. Box 240402
Memphis, TN 38124-0402
1-901-681-9938

Parents Choice
parentschoice@mailcity.com
733 Lupton Dr. #a
Chattanooga, TN 37415
1-877-657-4045

State of Franklin Homeschoolers
kramerbg@mounet.com
494 Mill Creek Road
Kingsport, TN 37664
1-423-349-6125

Tennessee Home Education Association
3677 Richbriar Court
Nashville, TN 37211
1-615-834-3529

TnHomeEd—Tennessee's Homeschool Information Site
Kay@TnHomeEd.com
3929 Ivy Drive
Nashville, TN 37216

Unschoolers of Memphis
mmyer@midsouth.rr.com
Memphis, TN
1-901-757-9859

TEXAS

Austin Area Homeschoolers
LADerrick2@aol.com
10213 Rhett Butler Dr.
Austin, TX 78739

HATCH (Houston Area Tri-County Home Educators)
hatch@pdq.net
P.O. Box 162
Cypress, TX 77433

Home Educators Alliance & Resources of Texas
heart@qzoneinc.com
Hidalgo County, TX

Home School Texas (HOST)
info@homeschooltexas.com
P.O. Box 29307
Dallas, TX 79536
1-214-358-2996

HomeNET Home School Association
gonfishn@risecom.net

P.O. Box 155
Gallatin, TX 75764
1-906-683-1399

Homeschooling with Special Needs Support Group
plato78610@yahoo.com
Austin, TX
1-512-243-0338

Houston Unschoolers Group
mhfurgason@hotmail.com
9625 Exeter Rd
Houston, TX 77093
1-713-695-4888

Minority Homeschoolers of Texas
president@mhot.org
P.O. Box 2322
Cedar-Hill, TX 75106
1-972-354-2520 Ext. 7693

North Texas Home Educator's Network
info@nthen.org
P.O. Box 830207
Richardson, TX 75083
1-806-744-4441

Southeast Texas Home School Association (SETHSA)
sethsa@sethsa.org
P.O. Box 692075-297
Houston, TX 77269
1-281-370-8787

UTAH

Charlotte Mason Study Group of the Salt Lake Area
PennyGar@aol.com
P.O. Box 900983
Sandy, UT 84090

LDS Home Educators Association
comments@ldshea.org
2770 South 1000 W
Perry, UT 84302
1-435-723-5355

Salt Lake Home Educators
shark@xmission.com
1-801-501-0344

Utah Christian Home School Association (UTCH)
utch@utch.org
P.O. Box 3942
Salt Lake City, UT 84110-3942
1-801-296-7198

Utah Home Education Association
P.O. Box 167
Roy, UT 84067
1-888-887-UHEA

VIRGINIA

Home Educators Assisting, Reaching, and Teaching (HEART)
BIZIMOM807@aol.com
101 William Clairborne

Williamsburg, VA 23185
1-757-220-2052

Home Educators Association of Virginia
HEAV33@aol.com
1900 Byrd Avenue, Suite 201
P.O. Box 6745
Richmond, VA 23230-0745
1-804-288-1608

Home Educators Network (HEN)
amjcsck@juno.com
9503 Treemont Lane
Fredericksburg, VA 22553
1-540-582-5031

HOPE (Home Organization of Parent Educators)
hope-hs@juno.com
14120 Walton Drive
Manassas, VA 20112
1-703-791-HOPE

LIFE (Learning in a Family Environment)
aagerhardt@aol.com
11465 Dutchman's Creek Road
Lovettsville, VA 20180

Mount Vernon Homeschoolers Association
halljeff@erols.com
9119 Volunteer Drive
Alexandria, VA 22309
1-703-799-9065

Roanoke Home Educators Network
vaplyers@aol.com

5731 Montague Way
Roanoke, VA 24018
1-540-989-3403

SEARCH—Southside Embracing All Religions in Homeschool
hauseraud@aol.com
2231 Beech Street
Virginia Beach, VA 23451
1-757-496-3964

SpringTree Home School Support Group
lowfog@earthlink.net
7120 Hadlow Court
Springfield, VA 22152

Virginia Home Education Association (VHEA)
info@vhea.org
P.O. Box 5131
Charlottesville, VA 22905

VERMONT

Center for Homeschooling
95 North Avenue
Burlington, VT 05401
1-802-862-9616

Christian Home Educators of Vermont
rebrobin@sover.net
146 Sherwood Circle
Brattleboro, VT 05031
1-802-254-7697

United Homeschoolers
dltimian@together.net
264 Tortolano Road
South Royalton, VT 05068
1-802-763-2837

Vermont Association of Home Educators
liberty@together.net
RR1 Box 847
Bethel, VT 05032
1-802-234-6804

Vermont Homeschoolers' Association
Rural Route 2, Box 4440
Bristol, VT 05443
1-802-453-5460

WASHINGTON

Busy Bee's Christian Homeschoolers
MelBx3@aol.com
Marysville, WA
1-360-657-7172

Family Learning Organization
homeschool@familylearning.org
P.O. Box 7247
Spokane, WA 99207-0247
1-509-467-2552

LEARN (Life Education Activity Resource Network)
LEARNatHomeFam@aol.com
P.O. Box 8783

Lacey, WA 98509
1-360-491-6234

Olympia LDS Home Educators
hanson01@home.com
P.O. Box 879
East Olympia, WA 98540

Peninsula Homeschool Exchange
dcarroll@cablespeed.com
419 Benton St.
Port Townsend, WA 98368
1-360-385-3830

Spokane County Homeschoolers Association
SoSpokaneCoHs@hotmail.com
P.O. Box 184
Mica, WA 99023
1-509-891-1370

Teaching Parents Association
info@washtpa.org
P.O. Box 1934
Woodinville, WA 98072-1934
1-206-505-1561

Washington Home Education Network
gardenfev@nwi.net
1-360-805-0770

Washington Homeschool Organization
WHOoffice@foxinternet.net
6632 South 191st Place, Suite E100
Kent, WA 98032-2117
1-425-251-0439

WISCONSIN

Dodge County Home Educators
Noel Eedy
755 East Center Street
Juneau, WI 53039
1-920-386-0387

H.O.M.E.
amckee73@hotmail.com
5745 Bittersweet Place
Madison, WI 53705
1-608-238-3302

Milwaukee Area Christian Home Educators
mache@quakkelaar.com
P.O. Box 1355
Menomon Falls, WI 53052
1-414-299-0985

Wisconsin Christian Home Educators Association
jang8@prodigy.net
2307 Carmel Avenue
Racine, WI 53405
1-262-637-5127

Wisconsin Latter-Day Family Home Educators
bzmom@geocities.com
P.O. Box 080853
Racine, WI 53408
1-414-637-4518

WEST VIRGINIA

Jackson County Homeschoolers
dweaver@alpha.wvup.wvnet.edu
P.O. Box 333
Cottageville, WV 25239
1-304-372-4333

Kanawha-Putnam Home Educators
P.O. Box 7541
Cross Lanes, WV 25652
1-304-766-9877

Morgan County Homeschoolers
zephyrs34@yahoo.com
1417 Fairfax Street
Berkeley Springs, WV 25411
1-304-258-5414

West Virginia Home Educators Association
mgmiller@citynet.net
P.O. Box 3707
Charleston, WV 25337
1-800-736-WVHE

WYOMING

Homeschoolers of Wyoming
mungermtrr@compuserve.com
P.O. Box 3151
Jackson, WY 83001
1-307-733-2834

APPENDIX C

*Summary of State Homeschooling Laws**

HOMESCHOOL REGULATION IS A RESULT OF compulsory school attendance laws, and each state's regulations are unique to that state. The National Home Education Network (NHEN), www.nhen.org, provides information about each state on its legal information Web pages. For each state, we include a brief overview of the law. From the NHEN Web site, these overviews are followed by links to relevant official documents, as well as links to state homeschool organizations that provide more detailed legal information. In the interest of brevity, we omit from the overviews the specific details about compulsory attendance ages and immunization requirements. All prospective homeschoolers need to read the fine print of the laws or regulations themselves, contact local support groups, and learn from homeschoolers in their state how the regulations actually work in practice. Experience shows us that often school officials seek to require more than is legally necessary or permissible. Homeschoolers must spend the time necessary to acquaint themselves with the complexities of the regulations.

*Courtesy of the National Home Education Network (NHEN), 2001. NHEN is a national organization that does an excellent job providing legal and legislative networking and information for the homeschooling community. Laws change rapidly. It is likely that by the time you read the information contained in this appendix, there will have been changes in laws that may govern your specific state. To assure yourself that you have the most current laws applicable to your situation, you should consult the NHEN Web site, at www.nhen.org, as well as the links included at the site. Local support groups can also provide resources, including attorney referrals, that can help you understand with confidence precisely what the requirements are, if any, that apply to your specific homeschool program.

CAUTION! Most state laws cannot be accurately summarized in a short paragraph. These overviews are only a starting place. You must spend the time necessary to acquaint yourself with the complexities of the regulations.

ALABAMA

Alabama does not recognize homeschooling as a separate legal option. Homeschoolers in Alabama educate their children according to the provisions set forth in certain laws and State Board resolutions that pertain to private schools in Alabama and, therefore, most find "covering" or "umbrella" church schools that will oversee their homeschooling programs. According to the attorney general of Alabama, "other than the state laws requiring parents to report attendance and for church schools to report if a student is no longer in attendance at such a church school, there is no provision in Alabama law that permits or requires any state or local authority to regulate a church school."

ALASKA

Alaska's compulsory attendance statutes do not apply if the child is "being educated in the child's home by a parent or legal guardian" [Sec. 14.30.010 (12)]. This exemption to the Compulsory Education Law allows children to be homeschooled by a parent or guardian without any state-mandated notification or testing.

ARIZONA

Arizona statutes require that every child of school age be taught at least the subjects of reading, grammar, mathematics, social studies, and science. The person who has custody of the child shall choose a public, private, charter, or homeschool to provide that instruction. For a homeschool, as defined in the statute, parents need to file an affidavit of intent with the county school superintendent stating that the child is being provided with instruction in a homeschool and including the child's name, date of birth, current address of the school the child is attending, and names, telephone numbers, and addresses of the persons who currently have custody of the child.

ARKANSAS

Parents are required to notify the local school superintendent of intent to homeschool by filling out a letter of intent and signing a waiver before August 15 or December 15 each year. Parents withdrawing children from public school during the school year must wait fourteen calendar days after filing the LOI to begin homeschooling. This requirement can be waived by the superintendent or school board. Testing is done in grades 5, 7, and 10. The homeschooled student must not be more than two years beyond the normal age for the appropriate grade. Students under disciplinary action or having excessive unexcused absences may not be allowed to begin homeschooling until they have met certain criteria.

CALIFORNIA

California has no specific homeschooling law and homeschoolers may choose one of five different legal options:

(1) private school independent study program
(2) establishment of a private school in one's own home
(3) public school independent study program
(4) charter school independent study program
(5) tutoring by a credentialed teacher (parent or other)

COLORADO

The Colorado general assembly has declared that it is the primary right and obligation of the parents to choose the proper education and training for children under their care and supervision. They further state that "non-public home-based education is a legitimate alternative to classroom attendance for the instruction of children and that any regulation of non-public home-based educational programs should be sufficiently flexible to accommodate a variety of circumstances." Home education is "subject only to minimum state controls which are currently applicable to other forms of non-public education."

CONNECTICUT

Connecticut statutes provide that parents shall instruct their school-age children or "cause them to be instructed in reading, writing, spelling, English grammar, geography, arithmetic, and United States history and in citizenship, including a study of the town, state, and federal governments." The Connecticut Department of Education has developed "procedures" for homeschoolers, but these procedures are not law, only "suggested."

DISTRICT OF COLUMBIA

There are no specific statutes dealing with homeschooling. Those homeschoolers who do report are those who are removing a child from school; then they simply file a notice of intent with the school department.

DELAWARE

Delaware provides an exemption from their compulsory attendance laws for "any student enrolled in a private school who is receiving regular and thorough instruction in the subjects prescribed for the public schools of the State in a manner suitable to children of the same age and stage of advancement." The statute further provides that private schooling, including "homeschools and homeschool associations" must report yearly to the Department of Education providing the "enrollment, age of pupils, and attendance." Homeschoolers may instead opt to report directly to the local superintendent, who "shall determine in writing that the student is or will be provided with regular and thorough instruction in the subjects prescribed for the public schools of the State in a manner suitable to children of the same age and stage of advancement."

FLORIDA

Florida statutes provide prospective homeschoolers three options. Homeschoolers may enroll in a private school that offers a homeschooling option and follow the procedures set by the school. Or they may establish a home education program as defined in the statutes by sending a Notice of Intent to their local school superintendent, maintaining a log of activities and samples of work, and filing an annual evaluation using one of five evaluation choices. Or they may hire a private tutor.

GEORGIA

Homeschooling in Georgia is defined in the Georgia Code. Homeschoolers must submit an annual declaration of intent to the local school superintendent. The teaching parent must have a high school diploma and may employ a tutor with at least a baccalaureate college degree. Subjects must include reading, language arts, mathematics, social studies, and science. There are requirements for the length of the school year and for reporting attendance monthly. The teaching parent must write annual progress reports, and standardized tests must be taken every three years beginning at the end of third grade; neither the progress report nor the test results are routinely submitted to local or state authorities.

HAWAII

Homeschoolers must file a notice of intent with the principal of the local public school. No approval is needed. The required "written record of the planned curriculum" is not ordinarily shared with the school. An annual progress report is required; progress may be shown through testing, evaluation by a certified teacher, or parent-written report providing statements of progress in each subject area and samples of the student's work. Standardized test scores are normally required in grades 3, 6, 8, and 10, but there are provisions for alternatives to standardized testing.

IOWA

Homeschoolers have four options to legally homeschool in Iowa. The first option is to work with a supervising teacher; the parent must have eight meetings, four of which must be face-to-face. The second option is to provide annually the results of a test administered by a certified teacher at the end of every school year; there is a specific group of tests that the state approves and testing cannot be done by the parent. The third option is to create a portfolio every year; the parent finds a portfolio evaluator, who must be a certified teacher, and the parent must keep samples of the child's work, and a record of activities. At the end of the year, these are reviewed by the evaluator. The final option is the homeschool assistance program and only the larger school districts offer these programs; this option is also known as dual enrollment.

IDAHO

Parents are required to ensure that children are instructed in the subjects required by law, but not required to send the children to school if the children are "otherwise comparably instructed." Homeschooled students are considered "otherwise comparably instructed."

ILLINOIS

Illinois homeschools are private schools as long as they comply with Section 26.1 of the Illinois state statutes. As established by the Illinois Supreme Court in People vs. Levison (1950), Illinois laws pertain to all schools, including private schools, and provide for certain subjects to be taught, in the English language. If contacted by state school officials, homeschoolers may respond in different ways, including submitting a typed and signed letter stating simply that the children are receiving private education as required by Section 26-1.

INDIANA

Indiana law requires homeschoolers to provide 180 days of instruction and keep attendance records, though there is no special form for these records, which are, as the code states, "kept solely to verify the enrollment and attendance of any particular child upon request of the state superintendent of public instruction." Homeschools must provide instruction equivalent to that given in the public schools, but, as stated on the DOE Web site, "state law does not define equivalency of instruction." Further, "state law exempts homeschools from the curriculum and program requirements which public schools must follow."

KANSAS

The Kansas compulsory attendance requirement can be satisfied at a public school or at a "private, denominational or parochial school," which also includes homeschools. The homeschool, like other private schools, must meet certain basic statutory requirements, such as "competent instructor" and "substantially equivalent" period of time. For legal purposes, homeschools in Kansas are considered nonaccredited private schools.

KENTUCKY

In Kentucky, homeschools operate as private schools. As such, they are not subject to rigorous government regulations. Each school year, homeschoolers simply send a letter of their intent to homeschool to their local public school district director of pupil personnel stating the names, ages, and place of residence of each child in attendance at the homeschool. In addition, each homeschool must keep attendance records, regular scholarship reports, and school a minimum of 175 days per year (1,050 hours). Approval from the public schools is not needed, and standardized testing and/or filing of report cards is not required. If a family begins homeschooling during the middle of a semester, they are subject to certain other procedures, listed in the Department of Education's "Best Practices" document.

LOUISIANA

In Louisiana the options when deciding to homeschool include registering as a private school or pursuing state-approved home study. For state-approved home study, homeschoolers follow the guidelines of the Department of Education. To choose the private school option, parents register with the state of Louisiana as a private school by sending in an annual letter of intent indicating the number of children enrolled.

MAINE

Homeschooling rules are found in Chapter 130, entitled Rules for Equivalent Instruction Programs, pursuant to 20-A M.R.S.A. 5001-(3) (A). Parents submit to the state Department of Education an application, which satisfies the compulsory school attendance laws. The application asks parents to choose their method of homeschool support, which can be another homeschool family with one year's experience, and to provide other basic information. Annual assessments may take a number of forms.

MARYLAND

Current regulations in Maryland provide flexibility for homeschoolers. To start, parents submit an Assurance of Consent form fifteen days before taking their child out of the school system. The law requires that parents provide "regular and thorough instruction" but does not specify what that entails. Thus there are no requirements such as a set number of days per year or hours per day. There are basically three ways to demonstrate compliance with the regulations: submit a portfolio for review, register with an approved satellite program, or register with an umbrella program.

MASSACHUSETTS

There is no statewide policy for homeschooling. Local school districts develop policies according to the guidelines set forth in two Supreme Judicial Court Cases, Charles and Brunelle, which list factors that school committees may consider when approving an education plan, but there is no one set of requirements. Any requirements for approval of the education plan must be "essential" ones. Various evaluation methods are possible.

MICHIGAN

For children being educated at home by their parents, an exemption from the requirement to attend public school may exist either under the nonpublic school provision or the home education provision. The nonpublic school provision, 3(a), provides for teaching subjects comparable to those taught in the public schools and comes under the jurisdiction of the state Department of Education. The home education provision, 3(f), provides for an organized educational program in the specified subject areas and comes under the jurisdiction of the local school district. In either case, there is no requirement to notify or seek approval of the state for the homeschool.

MINNESOTA

Parents wishing to homeschool their children annually report the names and birth dates of their children. If the parent does not have a baccalaureate degree, quarterly report cards must be submitted to the school superintendent. There is annual testing, with the method of administration mutually acceptable to both the parent and superintendent. Minnesota families are not required to provide test scores to superintendents. Parents must make available (not specified when or under what circumstances) documentation that required subjects are being taught.

MISSISSIPPI

The state has a minimal amount of regulation that families must follow to legally homeschool. A legitimate home instruction program is defined as one that is not "operated for the purpose of avoiding or circumventing the compulsory attendance law."

MISSOURI

Any parent may educate a child at home. The parent does not have to have a teaching certificate or meet any education requirements. The law is permissive in the area of registering. The statute says the parent "may" notify the superintendent of schools or the recorder of county deeds in the county where the parents reside. This is to be done before September 1 annually, but is not mandatory.

MONTANA

Annually notify the county superintendent. Key parts of the Montana state code are sections 20-5-102, 20-5-109, and 20-5-111. Section 20-5-109 covers nonpublic schools as well as homeschools, and includes requirements such as length of school year, maintaining immunization and attendance records, and providing regular instruction in basic subjects. Section 20-5-111 was written specifically about homeschooling, and states that a parent has the authority to homeschool and is solely responsible for the educational philosophy; the selection of instructional materials, curriculum, and textbooks; the time, place, and method of instruction; and the evaluation of the homeschool instruction.

NEBRASKA

Homeschools are considered private schools. Parents may educate their children at home by filing for an exemption from state requirements on the basis of either "sincerely held religious beliefs" (Rule 13) or because the requirements "interfere with decisions of the parents or legal guardians in directing their child's education" (Rule 12). Private schools are required to teach certain subjects and provide a certain length of term. Paperwork must be filed by August 1 or 30 days prior to the start of homeschooling. Parents must submit reliable proof of the child's identity and age.

NEVADA

Nevada law (NRS 392.070) provides for a waiver of the compulsory attendance laws if the parent or guardian provides written evidence to the local school district that their child will be receiving appropriate instruction at home. State regulations (NAC 392.015–392.075) describe the requirements for this written evidence. Homeschoolers are not required by law to use any particular form to provide the written evidence; however, sample forms are available from homeschooling groups in Nevada.

NEW HAMPSHIRE

To comply with the homeschooling statute in New Hampshire, parents send a) a letter of intent either before the first day of the new school year or when beginning a home education program, if later, and b) a description of the scope, sequence, and materials for the program within thirty days of the initial letter of intent. A portfolio containing samples of the child's work must be maintained, and some type of evaluation must be provided by July 1. Most homeschoolers choose portfolio evaluation, but the law indicates that "any mutually [between parent and administrator] agreed upon method" is acceptable. Additionally, New Hampshire has a dual-enrollment statute that allows for homeschoolers to participate in curricular and cocurricular (but not extracurricular) public school activities. Extracurricular activities are allowed at the discretion of the individual schools and superintendents.

NEW JERSEY

There is no statute that directly addresses homeschooling in New Jersey. The compulsory education law (N.J.S.A. 18A:38-25) requires parents of school-age children to cause them "regularly to attend the public schools of the district or a day school in which there is given instruction equivalent to that provided in the public schools [. . .] or to receive equivalent instruction elsewhere than at school." Homeschooling falls under "elsewhere than at school." "Equivalent" was held, in State v. Massa (95 NJ Super 382; 1967), to mean academically equivalent only—i.e., the same basic subject areas must be covered, but not necessarily in the same way as the schools cover them. School districts are not required or authorized to review curricula, test homeschooled children, or monitor their outcomes. Parents are not required by law to notify their public school district of their intention to educate the child elsewhere than at school. Practice has varied over the years, with some families notifying every year, some notifying only the first year, and some never notifying. Notification is recommended, as a courtesy, when removing a child from public school to begin homeschooling.

NEW MEXICO

As of June 2001, standardized tests are no longer required of homeschoolers in New Mexico. The only paperwork required is filing a notice of intent with the school district superintendent within thirty days of establishing the homeschool and by April 1 of each subsequent year.

NEW YORK

Homeschooling is regulated according to Section 100.10 of the regulations of the New York State Commissioner of Education. These regulations require that parents file a notice of intent to home instruct, an Individualized Home Instruction Plan (IHIP), and four quarterly reports during the school year. At the end of each school year, parents must submit the results of an annual assessment on each child. In some grades, the regulations require standardized tests; in other grades, parents may substitute a narrative report as an alternative assessment.

Homeschoolers must file these documents with their local school districts. School districts do *not* have discretionary authority to "approve" or "disapprove" an IHIP. School districts must deem an IHIP to be in compliance as long as it provides for a plan of instruction in each of the required subjects for the required number of hours (900 hours for grades 1–6; 990 hours for grades 7–12). School districts do *not* have the authority to require homeschoolers to submit any information beyond that required by the Section 100.10 regulations.

NORTH CAROLINA

Homeschooling is included under the existing private school law per a 1985 Supreme Court ruling and a 1988 statute. The director, or his staff, of the Division of Nonpublic Education has been designated to be the representative who accepts application (notice of intent) to open a homeschool, and is authorized to inspect the results of national standardized testing annually. An attendance record and immunization record must be maintained.

NORTH DAKOTA

Under North Dakota statutes, parents may legally fulfill the compulsory instruction requirements in a home education program "based in the child's home and supervised by the child's parent or parents."

OHIO

Homeschooling regulations are promulgated under the State of Ohio Administrative Code (OAC). Proper notification must be given to the superintendent each school year. Parents must meet minimum qualifications. Nine hundred hours of home education must be provided each year and include a number of specified subjects. An annual academic assessment report of the child is required and may consist of standardized testing, a written narrative, or other mutually agreed upon assessment.

OKLAHOMA

The Oklahoma Constitution Article XIII Section 4 on compulsory school attendance states that "the Legislature shall provide for the compulsory attendance at some public or other school, unless other means of education are provided, of all the children in the State who are sound in mind and body, between the ages of eight and sixteen years, for at least three months in each year." Legal requirements for homeschooling in Oklahoma consist of providing an education for school-age children that is in good faith and equivalent to that provided by the state for at least 175 days per year.

OREGON

Parents of school-age children who wish to homeschool are required to send a one-time notice of intent to their local Education Service District within ten days of beginning homeschooling. Homeschoolers take an approved standardized test in grades 3, 5, 8, and 10, except in certain cases. A Privately Developed Education Plan can be developed for learning disabled students for whom standardized testing is not an appropriate option.

PENNSYLVANIA

The Pennsylvania Homeschooling Act 169-1988 specifies that parents must submit a notarized affidavit of their intent to homeschool. Along with this affidavit, they must also submit medical forms and a list of learning objectives covering the required academic subjects. School officials do not have discretionary authority to approve or disapprove a family's homeschooling plans or practice. They have authority to rule only on the narrow question of whether or not the parents have submitted the paperwork required by the law. Parents must maintain a log of instruction (e.g., list of materials read) and daily attendance records, must have at least a high school education, and must arrange each year for an annual evaluation of the child's progress by a certified teacher or licensed psychologist of their own choosing. At the end of the school year, parents must submit the professional's written evaluation that their child has received an appropriate education along with a portfolio of the child's work for the school district's review. In grades 3, 5, and 8, the homeschooled child must take a standardized test, administered by anyone other than the parent of the child. Parents also have a second option for homeschooling: the private tutor provision. In this provision, the tutor must be a certified teacher. Parents need submit only evidence of the tutor's credentials and criminal record clearance.

RHODE ISLAND

At-home instruction is approved by the local school district. State law requires: attendance equal to that of public schools, the keeping of an attendance register, and teaching of specific subjects. Local school districts can require evaluation that accommodates the parent's preferences.

SOUTH CAROLINA

In South Carolina, there are three options for homeschooling. All require parents to have a high school diploma or GED. The first is under the direction of local school districts, with annual testing. The second option is to homeschool under the umbrella of the South Carolina Association of Independent Home Schools (SCAIHS). SCAIHS requires annual membership fees and annual testing as well as curriculum review. The third option provides homeschoolers the accountability they need through homeschool associations (not the same as a support group). There are many to choose from throughout the state. Under this option, annual testing is not required and all records are maintained by the parent. This option provides the most freedom and choices of all the homeschooling options. Parents may sign a form stating that they wish to waive kindergarten.

SOUTH DAKOTA

South Dakota state law regulates home schools under the alternative instruction statutes, SDCL 13-27. Each homeschool must apply for an exemption certificate from the school board in their district for children ages six through sixteen. (Kindergarten is not mandatory.) The school board is generally obligated to grant the request. Provisions include: not less than 175 instruction days per academic year, instruction in the basic skills of mathematics and language arts that lead to a mastery of the English language, nationally standardized achievement tests required for grades 2, 4, 8, 11, and no teacher certification required.

TENNESSEE

Homeschoolers in Tennessee may choose one of three options: (1) Register with the Local Education Agency (LEA) as independent homeschoolers. Parents must have a high school diploma or a GED; if homeschooling a high school student, a baccalaureate degree or a waiver is required. The LEA does not provide curriculum, does not have the authority to inspect the home or approve the curriculum or schoolwork, and requires only some basic information. Attendance and instruction is required for 4 hours per day for 180 days. Testing is required in 5th, 7th, and 9th grades. Certain subjects are required in high school. (2) Register with a Church Related School (CRS). Under this option, parents report only high school students to the LEA, and must have a high school diploma. A baccalaureate degree to teach high school is not required. There must be 180 days of teaching, but curriculum, hours, and testing are determined by the CRS. The child in this option is considered a homeschooler. (3) Register with a CRS as a "satellite" of their campus and the child can be educated at home by the parent. Parents do not need a baccalaureate degree to teach their high schooler. Curriculum, tests, and hours of instruction are determined by the CRS, but 180 days of instruction is required. The child in this option is considered "privately educated."

TEXAS

Homeschools in Texas are considered private schools, as outlined in the court case of Leeper v. Arlington ISD, and are exempt from compulsory attendance requirements if their homeschool is operated in a bona fide manner (not a sham or subterfuge), if they have a written curriculum from any source (including video or computer) that covers the five basic subjects of reading, spelling, grammar, math, and a course in good citizenship. Private schools are not regulated in Texas; the state constitution (Article 7 Sec. 2) only authorizes the legislature to establish and maintain public schools, not private or parochial schools. Parents are not required to file any papers or notify anyone that they are homeschooling their children in Texas. If the children are already enrolled in a public school, parents must withdraw the children from school so they will not be considered truant. Parents need no approval of the school district in order to withdraw their children from school to be homeshooled or attend a private school.

UTAH

The Utah State Law (Section 53-A-11-102 [b] [ii]) states that a home educator is to hold school for a certain number of days and hours, teach the subjects prescribed by law, and request an exemption from compulsory attendance from your local school district. There are no other statutory requirements.

VERMONT

If a parent chooses to enroll a child in a home study program, he or she must submit an enrollment notice every year and may complete the enrollment in several ways depending upon the homeschooling style. The curriculum may be submitted as a detailed outline or as a narrative, and one of six different methods may be used to fulfill the previous year progress assessment. For a child being enrolled for the first time and who has not attended a Vermont public school in the past, evidence needs to be submitted on whether the child is handicapped. Parents that homeschool a handicapped child may have to show how they will provide any necessary special services or adaptations. The enrollment notice does not need approval, but it must include everything required by law so that the notice is complete. Vermont does have a religious exemption waiver from specific requirements dependent upon the commissioner's determination that the educational purposes are being met.

VIRGINIA

Section 22.1-254 of the Code of Virginia provides options for home education, which include the general home instruction statute used by most Virginia homeschoolers, as well as the approved tutor provision, and a religious exemption to compulsory schooling. Under the general provisions, homeschoolers must notify their county superintendent annually of their intent to homeschool. They also must provide a curriculum description and evidence that the parent either has a baccalaureate degree from an accredited institution, is a teacher of qualifications prescribed by the Board of Education, has enrolled the child or children in a correspondence course approved by the Superintendent of Public Instruction, provides a program of study or curriculum which, in the judgment of the division superintendent, includes the standards of learning objectives adopted by the Board of Education for language arts and mathematics and provides evidence that the parent is able to provide an adequate education for the child. Evidence of progress (such as independent assessment, standardized test scores, or a portfolio review) must be submitted to the superintendent by August 1.

WASHINGTON

To homeschool in Washington, parents must comply with one of four options: (1) Be supervised by a certificated person a minimum of one contact hour per week. (2) Have forty-five college-level quarter credit hours or its equivalent in semester hours. (3) Complete a course in home-based instruction at a postsecondary institution or vocational-technical institute. (4) Have the local school superintendent deem you sufficiently qualified. Parents are required to: (1) File a declaration of intent at the proper time, (2) keep certain records to be forwarded to any other public or private school to which the child transfers, (3) have the child take a standardized test annually (those approved by the State Board of Education and given by a qualified person) or have the child evaluated by a certificated person currently working within the field of education, (4) provide instruction in the eleven required areas.

WISCONSIN

On or before October 15, each administrator of a home-based private education program is asked to submit, on form PI-1206, provided by the Department of Public Instruction, a statement of the homeschool's enrollment as of the third Friday of September. Be aware that this is *not* a registration process, but merely an affidavit that attests that the criteria of s.118.165 (listed below) has been met.

On this form you verify that the program of instruction is provided by the child's parent or guardian, or by a person designated by the parent or guardian, and meets the following criteria:

1. that the primary purpose of the program is to provide private or religious-based education
2. that the program is privately controlled
3. provides a minimum of 875 hours of instruction each year
4. provides a sequentially progressive curriculum of fundamental instruction in math, reading, language arts, social studies, science, and health
5. that the program is not operated or instituted for the purpose of avoiding or circumventing the compulsory school attendance requirement

The form recommends that records be maintained of student instruction time and course outlines to show a sequentially progressive curriculum. Please note, however, that there are currently no provisions in Wisconsin law for the disclosure of these records to any school district or state education entity. There are no testing requirements.

WEST VIRGINIA

West Virginia Code § 18-8-1 allows for home instruction so long as the parent(s) give the county board of education: (1) notice of intent to provide home instruction at least two weeks prior to withdrawing child from public school, (2) evidence that instructor(s) have at least the equivalent of a high school diploma, and formal education at least four years higher than the most academically advanced child to be instructed (four-year rule). (NOTE: This four-year rule has been waived until June 1, 2003), (3) annually by June 30 an academic assessment of the child.

WYOMING

In Wyoming, a home-based educational program must meet the requirements of a basic academic educational program pursuant to W.S. 21-4-101 (a)(vi). A curriculum is submitted to the local board of trustees each year, showing a "basic academic educational program" that provides a sequentially progressive curriculum of fundamental instruction in certain required subjects, but no home-based educational program is required to include in its curriculum any concept or topic or practice in conflict with its religious doctrines.

INDEX